DISCOVERING
ARIZONA

GIBBS·SMITH
PUBLISHER

Much of the text in *Discovering Arizona* was adapted from *Arizona!* by Jay J. Wagoner. Wagoner has had a keen interest in southwest history since he began interviewing pioneers as a teenager. A soldier in the Army Signal Corps in Europe during World War II, and later a Fulbright Scholar in Brazil, he was a career high school teacher and researcher for over 30 years. Called "an accurate historian and a lively writer" by the *Arizona Republic*, Jay Wagoner has published numerous articles and dozens of books.

Published by
Gibbs Smith, Publisher
P.O. Box 667
Layton Utah 84041
800-748-5439
www.gibbs-smith.com/textbooks

Managing Editors: Carrie Gibson, Susan Allen Myers, Aimee L. Stoddard
Assistant Editors: Ryan Carr, Jen Peterson, Courtney J. Thomas
Photo Researchers: Carrie Gibson, Aimee L. Stoddard

Book Design: Richard Elton
Cover Design: Alan Connell

Cover photo: Arizona Office of Tourism
Tear Drop Arch in Monument Valley

Printed and bound in China
ISBN 1-58685-215-9

12 11 10 09 08 07 06 05 04   10 9 8 7 6 5 4 3

This book is dedicated to
Jay J. Wagoner,
who has done much to teach
us about his beloved state, Arizona.

ABOUT THE REVIEWERS

Mary Dohrendorf earned her B.S. Degree in Elementary Education from Central Missouri State University and her M.A. in Elementary Education from Arizona State University. She has a total of over 24 years of teaching experience in grades one through five. She especially enjoys the fourth grade Social Studies curriculum that focuses on the beautiful state of Arizona.

James D. McBride holds a B.A. in Business from the University of Maryland, an M.A. in Secondary Education, an M.A. in History, and a Ph.D. in History all from Arizona State University. He has been teaching history since his retirement from the U.S. Air Force in 1967. In 1984 he accepted a position as Faculty Adjunct in the History Department at Arizona State University, a position he still holds. Most of his teaching career has been devoted to teaching Arizona history. He has presented papers at state, regional, and national conferences and has had several articles published.

Raymond Perry grew up in Tuba City, Arizona. He is a member of the Navajo Nation and has always had a great interest in the history of his people. Currently living in Albuquerque, he is the host of a television program, *Creator Connection,* that discusses the beliefs of the Navajo. Perry works as a representative for educational publishers. He holds a B.S. in Applied Management from the University of Albuquerque.

Barbara Prior has lived in Arizona for more than 30 years. She has taught fourth grade in the Scottsdale Unified School District since 1985. She earned her B.S. degree in Social Sciences from California State Polytechnic University, San Luis Obispo, and a M.A. in Education from Northern Arizona University in Educational Leadership.

Ellen S. Thomas earned a B.A. in Elementary Education and French Literature from the University of Detroit and a M.A. in Educational Administration from Northern Michigan University. She has taught in elementary schools for over 32 years. Besides teaching in Arizona for the past twelve years, she has taught in Denmark and Michigan.

Contents

Maps

Arizona State Symbols

Knowing our state symbols is a fun way to learn about Arizona. All the symbols show something special about our state. Arizona school children even helped choose some of our state symbols. They voted to choose our state reptile, amphibian, mammal, and fish. Can you tell what animals won their votes?

State Reptile: Arizona Ridge-Nosed Rattlesnake

This snake likes to hide in cool canyons of oak and pine trees. It is a small snake. A baby Arizona ridge-nosed rattlesnake weighs about as much as a quarter, and the adult snakes are not much larger than your arm. It likes to eat lizards and small mice.

State Mammal: Ringtail

When the first miners came to our state to find gold, silver, and copper, they also found a new friend—the ringtail! It was good at catching mice and became known as the "miner's cat." The ringtail stays awake at night and sleeps during the day. It has sharp claws and can leap between trees like a squirrel.

State Amphibian: Arizona Tree Frog

Not many states have a state amphibian, but we do! The Arizona tree frog has special pads on its toes to help it climb up trees. This frog likes to live in places where it is wet, and it likes to eat bugs.

State Fish: Apache Trout

This fish was found on the Fort Apache Reservation, and that is how it got its name. It likes to live in small streams. If you've ever seen an apache trout, you are lucky. There are not very many of them.

State Bird: Cactus Wren

State Flower: Saguaro Blossom

Our state bird and flower are good partners. As its name shows, the cactus wren likes cactus. It even builds its nests in cactus. Its song sounds like the "chug-chug-chug" of a car engine.

The saguaro cactus is the largest cactus in the United States. In the early summer, blossoms appear on the tips of its long arms. Bees and flies like the blossoms. Some Native Americans harvest the fruit and make it into syrup.

State Necktie: Bola Tie
State Gemstone: Turquoise
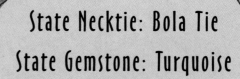

Not many states have a state necktie, but the bola tie is a good symbol for Arizona. A man in Wickenburg, Arizona created the tie. It can come in many shapes and sizes. One type has our state gemstone, turquoise. For a long time, Native Americans in the Southwest have used this blue-green stone for jewelry.

State Tree: Palo Verde

The Spanish name for our state tree means "green stick." That's a good name for this tree. Unlike most trees, the palo verde has green bark on its trunk. In the spring, the tree changes color and looks like gold. Have you seen a palo verde tree?

State Fossil: Petrified Wood

There is so much petrified wood in Arizona that we have a Petrified Forest! Long ago, this fossil used to be real wood. Over time, many layers of sand covered the trees. Slowly, the wood became more like rock than like wood.

State Flag

Our state flag is bright and colorful. The copper star is a symbol for our copper industry. As one person put it, the Arizona flag shows the "copper star of Arizona rising from a blue field in the face of a setting sun."

Arizona State Song

The song *Arizona* is one of our state's official songs. Rex Allen Jr., an Arizona native, wrote it. Read the words to the song and see how they describe our state.

I love you Arizona;
Your mountains, deserts and streams
The rise of Dos Cabezas*
And the outlaws I see in my dreams.

I love you Arizona,
Superstitions and all
The warmth you give at sunrise
Your sunsets put music in us all.

Oo, Arizona
You're the magic in me
Oo, Arizona
You're the life-blood in me.

I love you Arizona
Desert dust on the wind
The sage and cactus are blooming
And the smell of the rain on your skin.

Oo, Arizona
You're the magic in me
Oo, Arizona,
You're the life-blood in me.

*Dos Cabezas means Two Heads. They are
mountain peaks in Cochise County, Arizona

Chapter 1

"To see the earth as we now see it, small and beautiful in that eternal silence where it floats, is to see ourselves as riders on the earth together."

—Archibald MacLeish

Arizona's Place in the World

As seen from space, the earth looks like a big, blue marble in a black sea of sky. The shape of Arizona is not clear. To understand Arizona, we must look closer. We must find our place in the world and our country.

Mapping Arizona

PLACES TO LOCATE
North America
Canada
Mexico
California
New Mexico
Utah
Flagstaff
Phoenix
Tucson
Yuma
Mt. Humphreys

WORDS TO KNOW
climate
continent
country
elevation
geography
hemisphere
latitude
location
longitude
monsoon
pollution
precipitation

THE PLACE WE CALL HOME

Arizona seems very large, but it is just one small part of the world. We live in Arizona. It is important to us. It is our home. People all over the world live in places that are important to them.

We will learn about the *geography* of Arizona. Geography is the study of the land, water, plants, animals, and people of a place.

Where in the World is Arizona?

We live on the planet Earth. But just where on the earth can you find Arizona? On a globe or world map, we see seven large land areas. They are called *continents*. Arizona is on the continent of North America. Can you name the other six continents in the world?

North America is divided into *countries*. A country is a land area with its own government. Our country is the United States of America. The country south of us is Mexico. Which country is north of us?

Our country has fifty states. What states are our neighbors?

How Do We Find a Place?

Pretend you met someone from a different country, and they wanted to visit your home. How would you tell them where to find it? There are two ways we can describe a *location*.

Relative location tells us where a place is in relation to other places or things. For example, Arizona is *between* California and New Mexico. It is *south* of Utah. You could tell someone you live near the Colorado River, next to the school, or down the hall from your friend's apartment. What is the relative location of your school?

Exact location is the exact spot where a place can be found. An address is an exact location. What is the address of your house?

Where in the World Are We?

Our **world** is the planet Earth.

Our **continent** is North America.

Our **country** is the United States of America.

Our **state** is Arizona.

Arizona's Place in the World

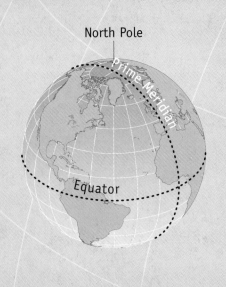

North Pole

Prime Meridian

Equator

LONGITUDE AND LATITUDE

You have an address at home. So does your school. *Longitude* and *latitude* lines are another way to describe a location. They are imaginary lines on a globe or a map. If you were to walk forever, you would never see a longitude line on the ground because they aren't real. If you were to walk over the line between Arizona and California, you wouldn't see that line either. The lines are only on maps.

Look at the globe. Find the equator. It is the imaginary latitude line that runs around the middle of the earth. Now find

Drawing Lines around the World

Look at this map of Arizona. You will see longitude lines that run up and down. Think of them as being "long." You will also see latitude lines that go from side to side. They run the same direction as the equator.

Find the numbers by the lines. Each number has a small symbol by it. The symbol stands for a degree. Latitude lines are named by how many degrees away from the equator they are. Can you guess how longitude lines are named?

Now, let's learn how to find a location. How far north of the equator is Tucson? Can you see that it is just north of the 32° line? How far north is Flagstaff?

Now, let's figure out Tucson's longitude. Can you see that it is almost on the 111° line? So, using the grid, Tucson's address is about 111° west longitude and 32° north latitude.

What is the address of Phoenix? What is the address of Flagstaff? Get as close as you can.

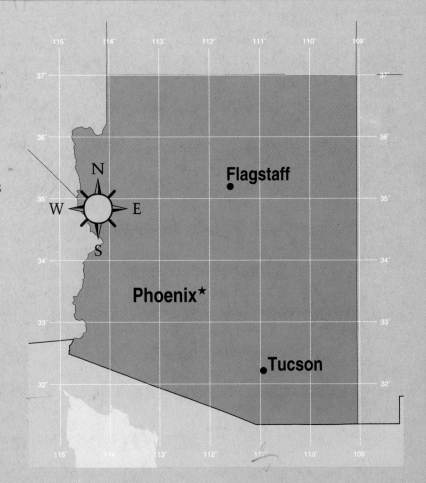

the prime meridian. It is the imaginary longitude line that runs from the North Pole to the South Pole. It goes through England and part of Africa.

Other longitude and latitude lines go north, south, east, or west of the equator and prime meridian. On a map, the lines cross each other to make a grid. Once you have the longitude and latitude of a place, you can use the grid to find an exact location anywhere on earth.

Hemispheres

There is another way we divide up the earth. We pretend that the earth is cut into two equal pieces. We call each half of the earth a *hemisphere.*

Look at these drawings of the earth. Find the equator. Find the hemisphere north of the equator. Find the hemisphere south of the equator. Since north is nearly always "up" on a map, it's not hard to guess that the hemisphere north of the equator is the Northern Hemisphere. What is the hemisphere south of the equator called?

Now, what if we decide to divide the earth another way? Geographers often divide it from the North Pole to the South Pole. The line runs through the Atlantic and Pacific Oceans. This drawing shows a Western Hemisphere and an Eastern Hemisphere.

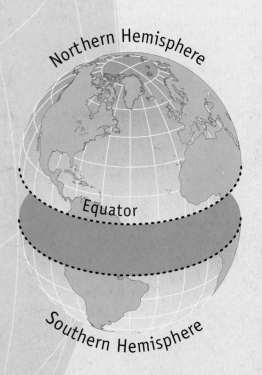

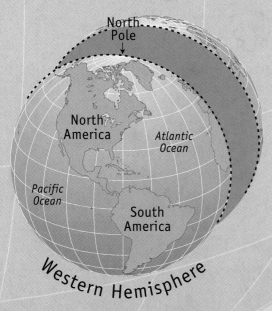

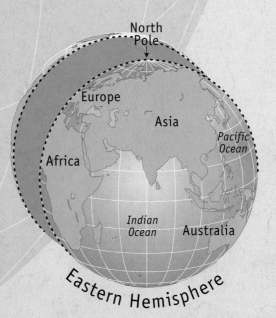

Climate and Weather

What's the difference between climate and weather? Each day's weather can be sunny or rainy, warm or cold, windy or calm. Climate is the weather of a place over a long period of time.

CLIMATE

Climate is important to a place. Climate is what the weather is like year after year. The amount of rain or snow that falls each year is part of the climate. The usual number of cold, warm, or very hot days each year are part of climate, too.

What makes the climate in one place different from the climate in another place? There are several reasons:

- **Distance from the equator:** The sun shines more directly on places near the equator, so they have a hot climate. The places farthest from the equator are cold all year long. They are close to the North and South Poles. The places in between are not always hot and not always cold.

- **Distance from large bodies of water:** The cold water of an ocean or lake helps cool the land nearby. When the water gets warmer in the hot summer, it helps warm the land in winter.

Large bodies of water also affect how much *precipitation* (rain or snow) the land gets. This is because water evaporates into the air, and then wind blows the moist air across the land.

- **Elevation:** "Brrr, the higher I go, the cooler the air," a hiker says. *Elevation* is how high the land is above the level of the ocean. The level of the ocean is called sea level. High places are usually cooler than lower places. This means that mountains are cooler than the valleys below. This is why some mountains have snow on the tops all year long.

ARIZONA'S CLIMATE

Arizona sometimes has the hottest and coldest temperatures in the United States on the same day. The White Mountains can be very cold. Desert towns along the Colorado River have hot summer days.

Nights in the desert can be cool. Clear skies let the heat float away. Nights in the big cities are warm. *Pollution* from cars is like a blanket that traps the heat. In the cities, there are a lot of cars that pollute the air. Cement, pavement, and brick buildings also hold a lot of heat that keeps the night air warm.

Rain and Snow

Arizona has two rainy seasons. During the winter, winds bring moisture from the Pacific Ocean. The rain falls slowly and soaks into the ground.

Late summer is *monsoon* season. Winds bring moist air across Texas from the Gulf of Mexico. There is a lot of thunder and lightning. Many inches of rain drop in a few minutes. Roads and rivers are flooded.

Winter snow falls in the mountains and on the high plateaus. In the spring, the snow melts. It runs into streams, and the streams run into rivers. The water is important for farms and cities.

• Humphreys Peak
12,633 ft

• Yuma, barely above
sea level

Mt. Humphreys is the highest point in Arizona. A place near Yuma is the lowest point. Which place would be colder? Why?

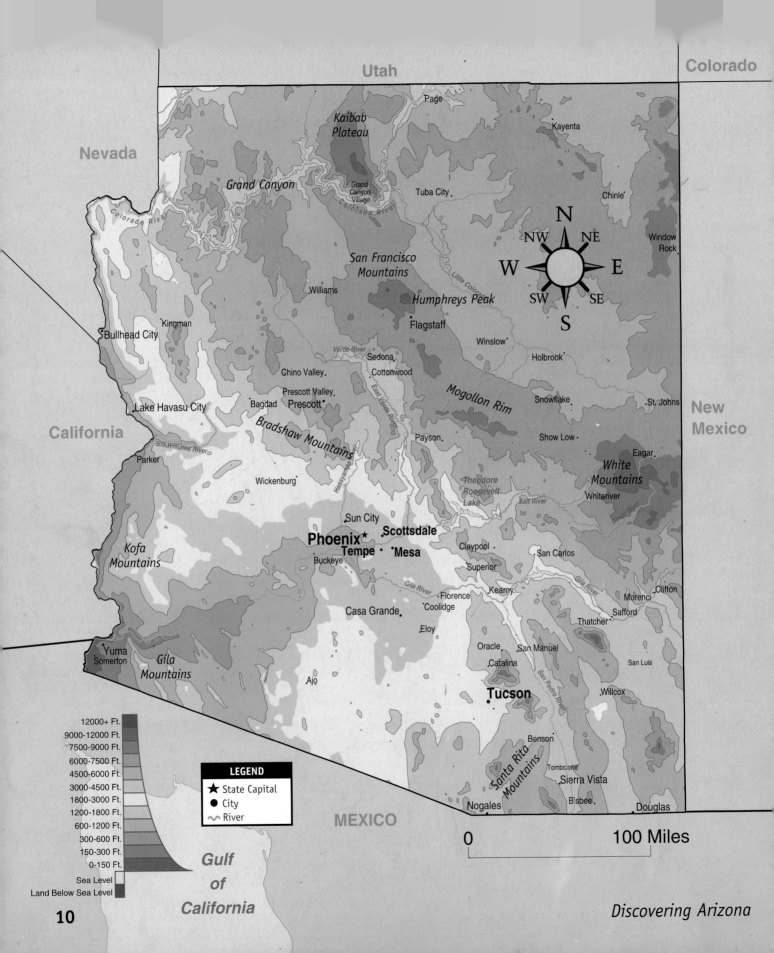

Utah

Colorado

Nevada

Kaibab
Plateau

Page

Kayenta

Grand Canyon

Grand
Canyon
Village

Colorado River

Tuba City

Chinle

San Francisco
Mountains

Window
Rock

Williams

Humphreys Peak

Little Colorado

Flagstaff

Winslow

Kingman

Bullhead City

Verde River

Sedona

Holbrook

Chino Valley

Cottonwood

Mogollon Rim

Snowflake

St. Johns

New
Mexico

Prescott Valley

Bagdad

Prescott

East Verde River

Payson

Show Low

Eagar

California

Lake Havasu City

Bradshaw Mountains

White
Mountains

Bill Williams River

Parker

Hassyampa River

Theodore
Roosevelt
Lake

Whiteriver

Wickenburg

Salt River

Black River

Sun City

Phoenix ★

Scottsdale

Claypool

San Carlos

Kofa
Mountains

Tempe

Mesa

Buckeye

Superior

Gila River

Kearny

Clifton

Morenci

Gila River

Casa Grande

Florence

Coolidge

Safford

Eloy

Thatcher

Yuma

Somerton

Gila
Mountains

Ajo

Oracle

San Manuel

San Luis

Catalina

San Pedro River

Tucson

Willcox

Benson

Santa Rita
Mountains

Tombstone

Sierra Vista

Nogales

Bisbee

Douglas

MEXICO

N
NW   NE
W   E
SW   SE
S

Discovering Arizona

LEGEND
★ State Capital
● City
~ River

12000+ Ft.
9000-12000 Ft.
7500-9000 Ft.
6000-7500 Ft.
4500-6000 Ft.
3000-4500 Ft.
1800-3000 Ft.
1200-1800 Ft.
600-1200 Ft.
300-600 Ft.
150-300 Ft.
0-150 Ft.
Sea Level
Land Below Sea Level

*Gulf
of
California*

0   100 Miles

Reading a Map

Maps help us understand where we are and how to find our way from one place to another. There are many different kinds of maps. There are city maps, maps that show mountains and rivers, and maps that show where important places are. Here are some things to look for when you read a map:

- **Compass Rose:** Most maps and globes have a compass rose. The four longer pointers on a compass rose show the four main directions: north, south, east, and west. The directions are called **cardinal directions**.

  Halfway between north and east is northeast, or NE. Southeast, or SE, is between south and east. These directions are called **intermediate directions**.

- **Legend or Key:** Mapmakers use symbols. An Arizona road map uses symbols for airports, parks, campgrounds, and other things. Most maps use the color blue for rivers and lakes. Some maps use colors to show elevation. A legend or key on the map tells what each symbol or color means.

- **Scale of Miles:** Some maps have a scale of miles to help us measure the distance between places.

0   50 Miles

Scale of Miles

Now that you know how to read a map, you can answer these questions:

1. What does SW stand for on a compass rose?
2. Using the legend, what is Arizona's capital city?
3. If you drove from Prescott to Phoenix, would you mostly be going uphill or mostly downhill?
4. How far is it from your town or city to Phoenix? What direction would you travel to get there?

Memory Master

Lesson 1

1. What is geography?
2. What do we call the lines on a globe or map that help us locate a place?
3. What three things most affect climate?
4. Where would you look on a map to see what a symbol stands for?

Lesson 2

Regions of the United States

PLACES TO LOCATE
the Midwest
the Northeast
the Southeast
the Southwest
   Gulf of Mexico
the West
   Pacific Coast states
   Rocky Mountain states

WORDS TO KNOW
human feature
lumber
natural feature
region
tourist

NATURAL AND HUMAN FEATURES

All places have certain features. Places can have different features or have features that are the same. Some of these are *natural features*. Soil, water, climate, plants, and animals are some natural features.

Places also have **human features** like cities, barns, homes, shopping malls, bridges, and roads. These are things that people have made.

WHAT ARE REGIONS?

The world we live in is very big. One way we can learn about our world is to think of it in smaller parts. We call these parts *regions*. A region is made up of places that have something in common.

What natural and human features do you see in these pictures?

Montezuma's Castle

A golf course near Tucson

Organ Pipe National Monument

Phoenix

Discovering Arizona

12

Many regions have the same natural and human features. There are regions where farmers grow cotton. There are regions where people work in tall office buildings. In some city regions, people may speak a different language.

A region can be big or small. A continent can be a region. Your neighborhood can be a region.

You can live in many regions at the same time. If you live in Phoenix, you live in a desert region. You also live in a *tourist* region. Many people come to visit each year. They spend money at hotels, restaurants, and national parks.

We can split the United States into many types of regions. Look at the map below. What are the five main regions?

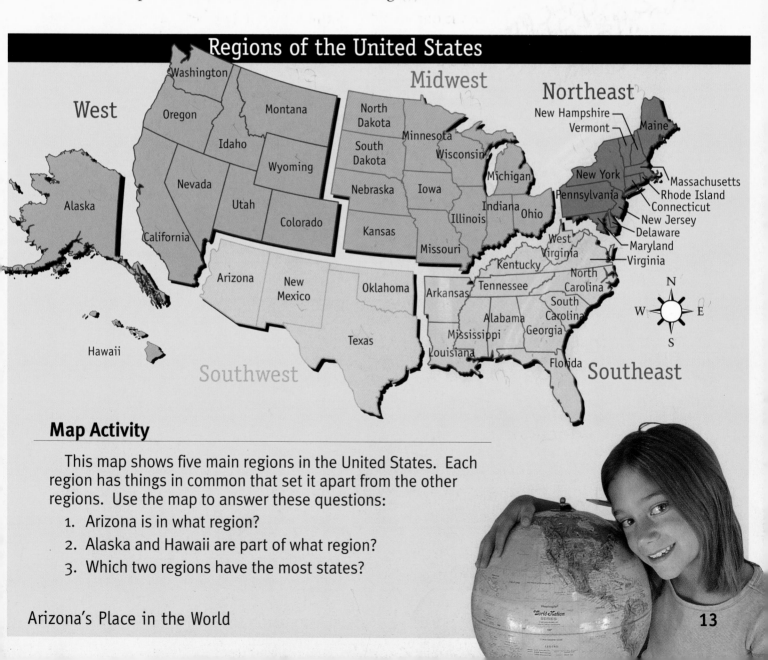

Regions of the United States

Map Activity

This map shows five main regions in the United States. Each region has things in common that set it apart from the other regions. Use the map to answer these questions:

1. Arizona is in what region?
2. Alaska and Hawaii are part of what region?
3. Which two regions have the most states?

LIFE IN THE WEST

The West is made of the Pacific Coast states and the Rocky Mountain states. The West is growing fast. Many people from Latin America and Asia are moving to Los Angeles, California, and the other big cities along the coast.

THE PACIFIC COAST STATES

California, Oregon, and Washington are three of the Pacific Coast states. The coast is rocky and beautiful in most areas. There are also large seaports, like Seattle, where people ship goods all over the world. Farmers grow fruits, grains, and vegetables. Washington apples and California avocados are sent to many places, including Arizona.

Climate

There is a lot of rain along the Pacific Coast, so these states have thick green forests. The forests are used for *lumber*. The temperatures are mild. Other areas are far from the ocean and get little rain. In these areas it can get really hot or really cold.

Plants and Animals

You can see many pine, spruce, cedar, and white oak trees if you visit this region. People grow tulips, roses, and other beautiful flowers. Wildflowers bloom in the spring.

Along the coast, salmon fishing is a big industry. In the Pacific Ocean, there are whales, dolphins, sea lions, crabs, and many kinds of fish. Eagles, hawks, and owls circle the skies.

These deer are getting their hooves wet in the cool Pacific Ocean.
Photo by Sunny Walter

Alaska and Hawaii

Alaska and Hawaii are also part of the Pacific Coast states. Alaska is huge! It is twice as big as Texas! People visit Alaska to hike, fish, and see nature. Alaskans are proud that their state has more elk, bears, and walruses than people!

Hawaii is a small group of islands in the Pacific Ocean. The rich soil and warm climate make Hawaii perfect for growing coffee, sugar, and pineapples. There are many ships in Hawaii's harbors. People go to Hawaii on vacation. They visit the ocean, beautiful beaches, mountains, and volcanoes.

Alaska

Hawaii

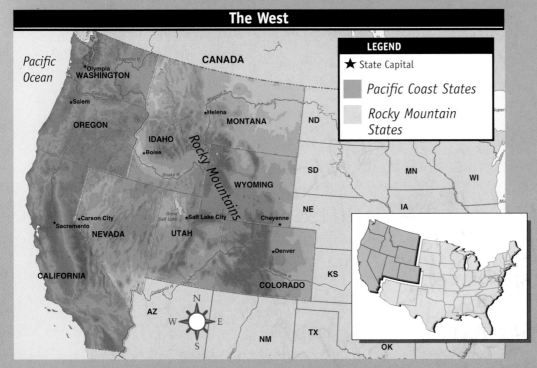

THE ROCKY MOUNTAIN STATES

The Rocky Mountain states are Idaho, Montana, Wyoming, Nevada, Utah, and Colorado. The Rocky Mountains stretch through most of this region. They are the longest mountain range in the United States. Many people like to spend time hiking, fishing, and camping in the mountains.

Cities like Las Vegas, Denver, and Salt Lake City are growing fast. Some people move there for work, and some move there because they like the climate.

Climate

The mountains get a lot of snow in the winter. People like to ski and snowboard. Mountain streams and rivers provide water for farmers. In the deserts, the summers are hot and dry. A cool summer rain shower is a welcome relief.

Plants and Animals

Aspen and pine trees cover the Rocky Mountains. People from all over the world come to Yellowstone National Park. It is one of the many places in this region to see wild animals like buffalo, bear, and elk. Hawks and eagles circle the skies.

In the deserts, you can see lizards, snakes, and insects keeping cool under rocks or plants. Watch out for a prickly cactus!

Bears live in the Rocky Mountains.

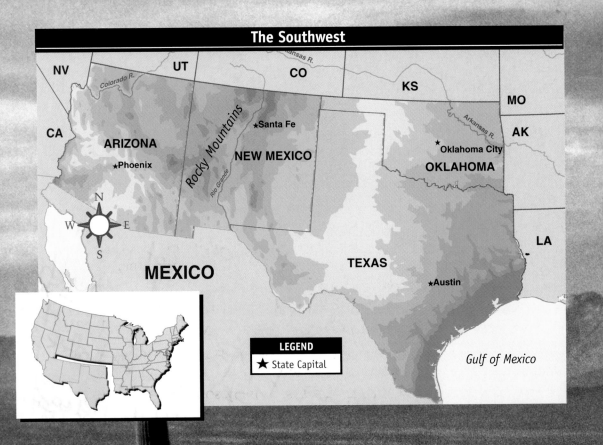

NV
UT
CO
KS
MO
CA
ARIZONA
Colorado R.
Rocky Mountains
★Santa Fe
NEW MEXICO
AK
★Phoenix
Rio Grande
Arkansas R.
★Oklahoma City
OKLAHOMA
N
W E
S
MEXICO
TEXAS
LA
★Austin
Gulf of Mexico

LEGEND
★ State Capital

THE SOUTHWEST

Arizona is part of the Southwest. New Mexico, Texas, and Oklahoma are also part of this region. The Southwest has high mountains and low deserts. This region has land of rugged beauty.

Cattle ranching and farming are important in the Southwest. Copper mining, manufacturing, and drilling for oil are also important in this region. Many people also work in electronics.

People like to visit places in the Southwest. They like the warm climate. The Grand Canyon is a popular place to visit. People also like to go to beaches along the Gulf of Mexico.

Today, the Southwest is growing fast. Many people are moving here from all over the country. They move to cities like Phoenix and Houston. Many Mexican Americans make their home in the Southwest. They come here for better jobs and opportunities.

16

Climate

In the desert, the land is dry. The air is dry, too. There are not many rivers, and there is not a lot of rain. Here summers are hot, hot, hot!

The mountains are cooler all year round. There are often afternoon thunderstorms in the summer. Where the mountains are high enough, snow falls in the winter.

Plants and Animals

You can see a lot of cactus plants and sagebrush in this region. If you look closely, you might spot an owl, roadrunner, or desert turtle. Watch out for rattlesnakes!

In the mountains, aspen and pine trees cover the land. Mountain streams are full of many kinds of fish. Moose, elk, and deer wander through the trees. In some places, there are mountain lions, bears, bobcats, and bighorn sheep. Have you ever heard a coyote howl at night? It is a lonely sound.

Four Corners

Two states from the Southwest and two states from the West are part of a special place. It is called the Four Corners. It is the only place in the United States where four states meet in the same place. Later, you will read about people who lived in this area long ago. Today, people visit the Four Corners. They can stand in all four states at the same time!

Utah

Colorado

Arizona

New Mexico

Lesson 2

Memory Master

1. What is a region?
2. What two groups of states are part of the West?
3. Arizona is part of what region?

Lesson 3

Other U.S. Regions

WORDS TO KNOW
blizzard
harbor
humid
prairie

LIFE IN THE MIDWEST

There is rich land and tall grass in the Midwest. It is some of the richest land in America. There are many wheat and corn fields. Cattle and sheep graze over the flat Great Plains that stretch from the Dakotas into Oklahoma and from the Rocky Mountains to the Mississippi River.

The Midwest is called the "breadbasket" of America. A lot of corn and wheat is grown in this region. The cereal and toast you eat probably come from this region.

Farming is still very important in the Midwest, but today most people live and work in cities. Detroit, Michigan, and Chicago, Illinois, are located on the Great Lakes. Chicago has the tallest skyscraper in the United States. It is the Sears Tower. People make a lot of cars in Detroit.

Climate

The Midwest can be very cold in the winter. Strong winds blow. *Blizzards* cover the streets with snow. In the spring, people who live near the rivers have to watch for floods. It is very hot in the summer. Sometimes strong winds or tornadoes blow over the plains.

What's in a Name?

A long time ago, most of the people in the United States lived along the coast of the Atlantic Ocean. They called places as far away as the Mississippi River "the West." Places in between were called "the Midwest."

Today, the states around the Great Lakes are still part of a region called the Midwest. They are not really in the middle of the West, but the nickname stuck.

The Mississippi River is the longest river in the United States.
Photo by Willard Clay

Discovering Arizona

Plants and Animals

The Midwest has prairie land. A *prairie* is wide grassy land with few trees. Prairie grasses and wildflowers are beautiful when they sway in the breeze.

Many animals live on the prairie. There are prairie dogs, deer, hawks, and jackrabbits. Much of the prairie land in the Midwest has been turned into farms and ranches.

Up north, there are woods and forests. Bears and skunks live there. Beavers and many kinds of fish live in the rivers.

There are many wheat fields in the Midwest.

Corn Power!

People are not the only ones who love corn. Corn is used to feed pigs, cows, and chickens. It is used to make corn syrup, cornstarch, and sugar. Corn oil is used for cooking and making paint, soap, and other products. Some corn is shipped to other countries to be sold.

Can you think of other ways we use corn?

LIFE IN THE SOUTHEAST

The Southeast has low mountains and rolling hills. It has coastlines and plains. The Atlantic Ocean is on one side. The Gulf of Mexico makes another border.

The Appalachian Mountains extend from Canada to Alabama. They have many forests and lakes. There are rivers, hills, and fields. People like to hike on trails in the Appalachian Mountains.

The Southeast also has great *harbors.* A harbor is a protected part of a body of water. Ships can anchor there. People use the harbors for trade. They send their crops around the world. New Orleans is a very important shipping port in the Southeast. The Mississippi River also helps in trade. Boats can take their cargo up and down the river.

There are large cities like Atlanta, Georgia, and small towns in the South, too. Many people make products in factories. Much of the land in the Southeast is good for growing crops. Farmers grow tobacco, rice, cotton, sugar, fruits, and nuts. Have you ever had a juicy Florida orange?

The South is famous for its music. Jazz, blues, and country music are very popular. People come to New Orleans to hear jazz performances. Have you ever listened to jazz music?

"A Southerner talks music."

—*Mark Twain*

In the Southeast, you can go for a ride on a paddle boat on a river.
Photo by Richard Cummins

Discovering Arizona

Climate

The Southeast is warm most of the year. It is often *humid.* That means there is a lot of water in the air. Some parts get a lot of rain. Some are drier.

Many birds come to the Southeast to escape the cold winters up north. So do people! They love to soak in the warm sun at beaches in the Southeast.

Plants and Animals

In the wetter areas, there are trees and swamps. The Southeast has pine, oak, walnut, beech, and cypress trees. Bright azaleas, violets, mountain laurels, and other wildflowers bloom in the spring.

Shrimp, clams, oysters, and catfish live in the water. Alligators and snakes live in the swamps. Cardinals, robins, and blue jays fly through the air. Bears, deer, skunks, foxes, and lizards are just some of the other animals that make their homes in the Southeast.

The Southeast

LEGEND
★ State Capital

IA
KS
OK
TX
MO
IL
IN
OH
PA
NJ
DE
MD
IL
Frankfort ★
KENTUCKY
WEST VIRGINIA
★Charleston
VIRGINIA
★Richmond
Nashville ★
TENNESSEE
Appalachian Mountains
★Raleigh
NORTH CAROLINA
ARKANSAS
★ Little Rock
MISSISSIPPI
Jackson ★
SOUTH CAROLINA
★Columbia
★Atlanta
GEORGIA
LOUISIANA
Baton Rouge ★
ALABAMA
★Montgomery
Atlantic Ocean
Gulf of Mexico
★ Tallahassee
FLORIDA

N W E S

Ohio R.

How would you like to meet this alligator face to face?
Photo by Richard Cummins

LIFE IN THE NORTHEAST

The Northeast is next to Canada and the Atlantic Ocean. It has deep harbors along the ocean. The harbors at Philadelphia, New York City, and Boston are busy places. Many ships take goods around the world.

The river valleys in the Appalachian Mountains are good for growing crops. Farmers grow corn, barley, and apples. They raise cows for milk and cheese.

The Northeast has oil, coal, and iron. Long ago, people came from all over the world to work in the mines, shops, and factories. They still do!

"Fish farming" is a growing industry. Fish farms in Maryland raise oysters, scallops, catfish, and trout. People in Maine fish for salmon and cod.

Climate

The Northeast has four seasons. In the fall, red, orange, and yellow leaves float down from the trees. You can rake them into a pile and jump in! The sky is often blue. The air is crisp and cool.

The winters are cold and wet. Sometimes there are ice storms. In the spring, bright green buds come out on all the trees. The summers are hot and humid. Many people go to the beach to feel the ocean breeze.

Have you ever eaten cod?
It is caught in the Atlantic Ocean.
Photo by Kindra Clineff

Discovering Arizona

Plants and Animals

What kinds of plants grow in the Northeast? On the coast, there are tall grasses. In the forests, there are many trees and wildflowers. Wild blueberries grow in the mountains. They are a good treat to eat on hikes.

Seagulls and other water birds fly above the shore. There are lobsters and clams along the shore, and cod and other fish swim in the ocean and rivers.

In the woods, there are black bears, deer, rabbits, and many other animals. Have you ever heard wild geese honk on their way south for the winter?

The Northeast

LEGEND
★ State Capital

CANADA
MAINE
VERMONT
★Augusta
Montpelier★
Concord★ NEW HAMPSHIRE
Lake Huron
Lake Ontario NEW YORK
Albany★ ★Boston
MASSACHUSETTS
Hartford★ ★Providence
RHODE ISLAND
Lake Erie CONNECTICUT
PENNSYLVANIA
Harrisburg★ Trenton★ NEW JERSEY
OH Ohio R.
Annapolis★ Dover★
Washington D. C. DELAWARE Atlantic Ocean
MARYLAND
WV
KY VA
Appalachian Mountains

How many fall colors do you see in this picture?
Photo by William H. Johnson

Lesson 3

Memory Master

1. Choose one of the regions from this lesson. Name two natural features and two human features in the region.
2. What is one of the main crops grown in the Midwest?
3. Describe the climate of the Southeast.
4. Name an important industry in the Northeast.

What's the Point?

Where in the world is Arizona? With the help of maps, we can locate our state. We can find places and measure distances on maps. We can also tell the elevation of a place.

Regions help us learn about the United States by dividing it into smaller parts. They help us see how places are alike or different.   We learned about five main regions in the United States. They are: the West, the Southwest, the Midwest, the Southeast, and the Northeast. Arizona is part of the Southwest region.

Activity

Making the Earth Flat

How is a globe different from a flat map? Slice an orange into four equal parts. Carefully peel the orange. Flatten out the peeling and lay them side by side. There are large spaces between the sections of the orange.

What does a mapmaker do to make a flat map from a globe? What will a mapmaker need to do with the split areas by the North Pole and the South Pole to turn a globe into a flat map?

On a flat map, why do Greenland and other land areas near the poles look much larger than they really are?

Activity

Regions and You!

1. Think about your school. Does it have its own regions? It probably has a gym or playground. It has an area where you eat lunch. It has rooms where you sit at your desk and learn. In each region, you do certain things. What other regions are in your school?

2. What kinds of regions are in your home? Make a map of your home. On the map, show what activities are done in each region.

The Southwest

Study this map of the Southwest region. Then close this book. From your memory, draw your own map of the Southwest on a large piece of paper. Make sure to label the names of the four states that make up this region.   If you remember the names of the state capitals or rivers, you can label them, too.

Then look in magazines, newspapers, or on the Internet for pictures of the Southwest. Find pictures that tell something special about life in this region. They could show some of the industries that are important. You might find pictures of places people visit in the Southwest, or you might find a picture of a big desert thunderstorm.   You could also use pictures of the many plants and animals that live in the Southwest.

Find at least one picture for each Southwestern state. Paste the pictures on the paper with your map. Write a sentence that explains each picture. Then share your pictures and map with your class or family.

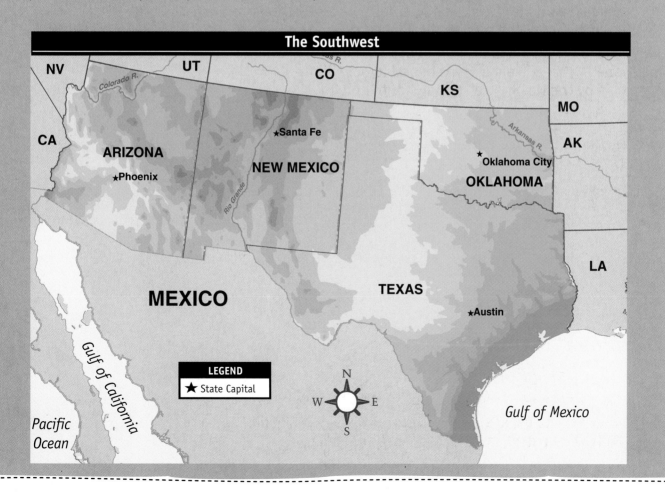

The Southwest

"I think that it is very deep and grand and that it must have taken a very long time to make it."

—*a young visitor to the Grand Canyon*

Chapter **2**

Beautiful Arizona

For millions of years, the winding Colorado River has cut deeper and deeper through the colorful rock layers of the Grand Canyon. In some places, the rocks are some of the oldest on the earth. If you visit the Grand Canyon, you can stand on the edge and look down into a slice of history.

Photo by Tom Till

MILLIONS OF YEARS AGO

Geologists have learned that long ago our land was different from what it is now. Geologists are scientists who study layers of rock to learn more about the past. They study how water, wind, and temperature have changed the rock.

When geologists find seashells in a layer of rock, they know that a sea once covered that land. A great sea once covered most of the land we know as Arizona. Arizona was underwater for millions of years. Small animals and fish died and left their shells and bones behind. The seas dried up and then came back over and over again.

The bottom of the sea was covered with *sediment.* The sediment was made of gravel, sand, mud, and shells of tiny sea animals. Later, the sediment changed into rock. *Sedimentary rock* was formed.

When the land was still very wet, plants and animals lived in swamps. When they died, they sank to the bottom of the swamps and were buried. This happened over many years. Coal formed deep under the ground from swamp plants. The ground moved and cracked. Sea water left minerals such as copper and gold in the cracks. Today, we mine the coal, copper, and gold from the ground.

Mountains and Plateaus

Pressure from inside the earth pushed up mountains and *plateaus.* A plateau is an area of high flat land that is many miles across. Wind and water cut down the mountains and plateaus. To make the land we see today, other mountains were formed by volcanoes. Hot lava flowed from volcanoes.

The land changed in other ways, too. Earthquakes made cracks in the earth. Rainwater and melted snow formed rivers.

Arizona Long Ago

PLACES TO LOCATE
Page
Wikieup
Grand Canyon
Keams Canyon
San Pedro Valley
Sonoran Desert

WORDS TO KNOW
extinct
fossil
geologist
glacier
plateau
sediment
sedimentary rock

Lesson 1

Discovering Arizona

Ancient Animals

Many kinds of animals roamed our land. Dinosaurs were huge reptiles that once walked through the swamps in Arizona.

There were dinosaurs that ate plants and dinosaurs that ate meat. Many plant-eating dinosaurs had long necks and very small brains. Why do you think they had long necks? Many meat-eating dinosaurs had sharp teeth and claws.

After a long time, the dinosaurs became *extinct*. They all died and never lived on the earth again. People have discovered their bones and tracks in many parts of the United States. Today, you can see dinosaur tracks on the Hopi Indian Reservation. The footprints come from a dinosaur that had three toes.

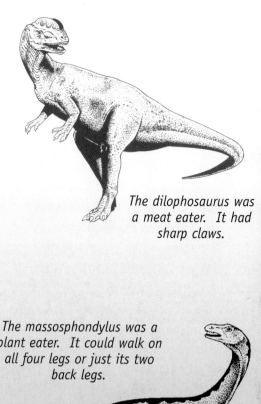

The dilophosaurus was a meat eater. It had sharp claws.

The massosphondylus was a plant eater. It could walk on all four legs or just its two back legs.

The diplodocus was a plant eater. It used its long tail as a weapon.

Have you ever seen a dinosaur's footprint? This one is near Page, Arizona.
Photo by Breck P. Kent

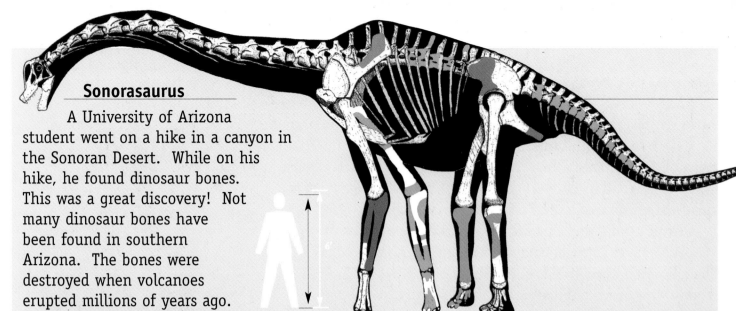

Sonorasaurus

A University of Arizona student went on a hike in a canyon in the Sonoran Desert. While on his hike, he found dinosaur bones. This was a great discovery! Not many dinosaur bones have been found in southern Arizona. The bones were destroyed when volcanoes erupted millions of years ago.

Scientists worked carefully to remove the bones from the site. Then they fit the bones back together. It was like trying to put together a great big puzzle with some of the pieces missing. A model of the Sonorasaurus is at the Arizona-Sonora Desert Museum in Tucson.

The dinosaur is named Sonorasaurus after the Sonoran Desert. Can you figure out how tall the Sonorasaurus was?

Fossils

Fossils are shells, bones, and other traces of a plant or animal in rock. Trilobites, shellfish, and other sea life have been found at the Grand Canyon. The land was once under water. Trilobites are small—about one to three inches long. At the canyon, geologists have also found fossils of a fish that looked like a shark.

Trilobite

Ammonite

The Ice Age

Long before any people lived in North America, a sheet of ice formed in Canada. As the air got colder and colder, the ice got thicker. In some places, it was over a mile thick. Huge sheets of ice called *glaciers* moved over Canada and the northern part of what is now the United States. The glaciers never reached as far south as the land we now call Arizona, but they did affect the weather here. Temperatures got colder and more rain fell. There were many green plants for animals to eat.

Discovering Arizona

Ice Age Animals

Camels, antelopes, and small horses lived here. Large bison, ground sloths, and tapirs lived all over North America. A tapir looks like a pig.

Huge mammoths were still here when the first people came. Mammoths were much larger than today's elephants. They could be fourteen feet tall. Some had long shaggy fur. The people hunted mammoths for food. Mammoth bones have been found with arrow points stuck in them.

Many mammoth skeletons have been found in the Southwest.

Giant Camels

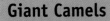

Camels lived in North America for millions of years. They were small at first, but later grew to be very large. Bones of giant camels have been found at Keams Canyon, the San Pedro Valley, and near Wikieup.

Keams Canyon •

• Wikieup

San Pedro • Valley

Bison

Lesson 1

Memory Master

1. How do geologists know that Arizona was once covered by a sea?

2. How did glaciers affect the weather in what is now Arizona?

3. Name two Ice Age animals that once lived in Arizona.

Lesson 2

Regions of Arizona

PLACES TO LOCATE

Plateau Region
  Canyon de Chelly
  Grand Canyon
  Meteor Crater
  Monument Valley
  Mt. Humphreys
  Petrified Forest
  Sunset Crater
  Mogollon Rim
Mountain Region
  Rocky Mountains
  Mt. Graham
  Mt. Lemmon
  Gila Valley
  Bisbee
  Globe
  Jerome
  Morenci
  Safford
  Sierra Madre Mountains
  Tombstone
Desert Region
  Sonoran Desert Region
  Phoenix
  Tucson
  Yuma

WORDS TO KNOW

canal
crater
erupt
meteorite
retire

Arizona's Land

From an airplane today, we can see three very different kinds of land in Arizona. Our state is divided into the Plateau Region, the Mountain Region, and the Desert Region. These regions were named for the kind of land found in each area.

Plateau Region

The Plateau Region is part of the Colorado Plateau. This larger region covers parts of Utah, Colorado, New Mexico, and Arizona. The plateau was lifted up when the earth was changing millions of years ago.

The Colorado and Little Colorado Rivers have cut deep canyons into the plateau. Mt. Humphreys is the highest peak

Arizona's Land Regions

Plateau Region

Mountain Region

Desert Region

Mountain

Desert

32

Discovering Arizona

in this region and in Arizona. The Mogollon (MUH-gee-own) Rim marks the plateau's southern edge. It is a steep rock cliff.

Lumber is important in the forests of the Plateau Region. People make money by cutting down trees to sell for wood. Cattle and sheep ranching are important. Some people work on the Santa Fe Railroad. Others mine coal.

Tourists come to the Plateau Region for a vacation. They come from all around the world to see the Grand Canyon, Sunset Crater, Meteor Crater, Petrified Forest, Monument Valley, and Canyon de Chelly. People also visit the Lowell Observatory near Flagstaff. They see the huge telescopes scientists use to study space.

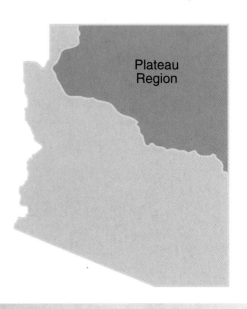

Plateau Region

Plateau

Beautiful Arizona

Arizona's Natural Wonders

Grand Canyon

Arizona is known as the Grand Canyon State. People from all over the world come to see the Grand Canyon. The Grand Canyon is one of the world's most famous natural wonders.

For millions of years, the Colorado River has been cutting this giant canyon deeper and deeper. Layers of different colored stone on the sides show how the earth has changed. At the bottom of the canyon, scientists have found fossils of the first living things on the earth.

The Colorado River looks very small in the valley of the Grand Canyon.
Photo by Steve Mulligan

Sunset Crater

Sunset Crater was the last of many volcanoes in the Flagstaff area to *erupt.* It erupted a thousand years ago. Black lava spread over hundreds of miles. Now, tourists can see the rim of this old volcano up close. The rim is an orange-red color.

Sunset Crater has not erupted for a long time.
Photo by James P. Rowan

Petrified Forest

The Petrified Forest is near Holbrook. Millions of years ago, large trees were washed downstream and buried. Iron, copper, and other minerals soaked into the wood. The trees turned into stone. The Petrified Forest National Park is part of the colorful Painted Desert. The Painted Desert is a large land area that has brightly colored sand and stone.

Discovering Arizona

Meteor Crater

Thousands of years ago, a huge *meteorite* slammed into the earth. The crash of this huge rock from outer space made a big *crater* in the earth. A crater is a big hole in the ground. Astronauts have trained here to learn how to walk on the moon. The moon has a lot of craters.

Meteor Crater is a huge hole in the earth. Astronauts have trained here to walk on the moon.
Photo by Eliot Cohen

In Monument Valley, you can see rock that has been shaped by the wind.
Photo by Steve Mulligan

Monument Valley

Monument Valley is a quiet, beautiful place on the Navajo Reservation. There are many large red rock formations called monuments. They are rocks carved by the wind over a very long time. They have names like Rooster Rock, Totem Pole, Elephant Rock, and the Three Sisters.

MOUNTAIN REGION

The Mountain Region is a link between the Rocky Mountains in Utah and the Sierra Madre Mountains in Mexico. There are about thirty different mountain ranges in this region. The peaks are covered with pine trees. The White Mountains are a popular place to hike and play in the winter snow.

Mt. Graham is the highest peak in the Mountain Region. It towers above the town of Safford in the Gila Valley below. Fir and spruce trees grow on Mt. Graham. Red squirrels live there. There are not many red squirrels left in the world. Scientists work at two large telescopes on top of Mt. Graham. They study the stars and planets.

Mt. Lemmon is close to Tucson. This mountain is a popular place to ski in the winter. People go there in the summer to hike, fish, or just cool off. Sunrise Park Resort in McNary is another popular place for skiing. People visit Sedona to see the red rock formations.

The Gila River and the Salt River have cut deep channels through the mountains. Arizona's best grazing land is here in the valleys. There are many cattle ranches.

Many towns in this region sprang up near copper, silver, and gold mines. Bisbee, Tombstone, Morenci, Globe, and Jerome are just a few of them.

Mountain
Region

Forests in the Mountain Region are beautiful places to cool off.
Photo by Willard Clay

Beautiful Arizona

Desert
Region

What do you think?

Before people came to live in Arizona, one man said, "Not even a wolf could live in this desert!" What do you think he would say now?

DESERT REGION

Most Arizonans now live in the warm, dry Desert Region. Thousands of people come here to *retire*. The Desert Region is part of the larger Sonoran Desert Region that stretches into Mexico. The desert has wide valleys bordered by mountains.

Desert plants and animals live in the Desert Region. The valleys have rich soil. Cotton, alfalfa, wheat, fruits, vegetables, and nuts are grown here. However, not much rain falls in this region. Water must be brought in from the mountains in wide *canals*. A canal is a waterway made by people. Other water is pumped up from under the ground.

Phoenix, Tucson, Yuma, and other cities and towns are in the Desert Region.

The Tucson Mountains are famous for a forest of saguaro cactus. Giant saguaro cactus live only in a few places of the world. They can live in our hot dry deserts because they store water during the rainy season. Saguaro can live for over 150 years. You can walk among the saguaro and many other cactus plants at Saguaro National Monument near the Mexican border.

Phoenix is a city in the Desert Region. It is growing fast.
Photo by Richard Cummins

A Desert Sunset

Over 100 years ago, John Van Dyke set out with his pony and his dog. At night, he watched the sunset. He wrote about what he saw.

Read this paragraph he wrote about the desert at sunset. Talk with your class about any words you don't know. Answer the questions that follow.

> A dusk is gathering on the desert's face, and over the eastern horizon the purple shadow of the world is reaching up to the sky. The light is fading out. Plain and mesa are blurring into unknown distances, and mountain ranges are looming dimly into unknown heights.
>
> Warm drifts of lilac-blue are drawn like mists across the valleys; the yellow sands have shifted into a pallid gray. The glory of the wilderness has gone down with the sun. Mystery—that haunting sense of the unknown—is all that remains.
>
> —John Van Dyke

1. How many colors does Van Dyke see in the desert sunset? What are they?
2. Why do you think the desert was a "mystery" after dark?
3. Have you ever watched a sunset? Write a paragraph about it. Use colorful words like this author did.

Photo by Willard Clay

Lesson
2

Memory Master

1. Name Arizona's three land regions.
2. List three of Arizona's natural wonders.
3. In what region do most Arizonans live?

Plants and Animals

PLACES TO LOCATE
Canada
Flagstaff
Fort Apache Reservation
White Mountains

WORDS TO KNOW
chaparral
habitat
hibernate
nectar
poisonous
reptile
timber

PLANTS IN ARIZONA

Many kinds of plants grow in Arizona. More than half of them are found in the desert.

Plants in the desert don't need much water. The desert palo verde is our state tree. The name means "green stick." In the spring, the palo verde is covered with beautiful yellow flowers. Some people grow palo verde, mesquite, and other desert trees in their yards. They don't need as much water as green lawns.

Cactus plants come in all sizes, shapes, and colors. The huge saguaro stores water during the rainy season. It grows slowly. It is found only in this part of the world. Its white blossom is our state flower.

During the spring, desert wildflowers bloom. Golden Mexican poppies, blue lupines, purple owlclover, and other flowers last only a few weeks. People come to enjoy the flowers.

Saguaro blossoms are our state flower.
Photo by LaVelle Morris

The Palo Verde is our state tree.
Photo by James P. Rowan

Discovering Arizona

Grasslands and Woodlands

Pretend you are in a car, traveling from the desert to the mountains. As you travel higher, the temperature drops. The desert turns into grasslands. Shorter grass and sagebrush grow on the high plateau desert.

As you climb higher, you see *chaparral* between the grasslands and forests. This is an area of small trees and thorny shrubs. Scrub oak is found in the woodlands. The evergreen juniper can be used for fence posts. Many people love the taste of yummy nuts from pinyon trees.

Forests

Keep climbing higher and higher. You will reach the forests. Trees that grow way up north in Canada also grow here. In Arizona, every 1,000 feet you climb is like moving 300 to 500 miles toward the North Pole!

The main *timber* tree in Arizona is the ponderosa pine. Timber is wood that is used to make things. Can you think of some products that are made of wood? The largest ponderosa pine forest in the United States stretches from Flagstaff to the White Mountains.

Quaking aspen and Douglas fir trees grow in Arizona's forests.

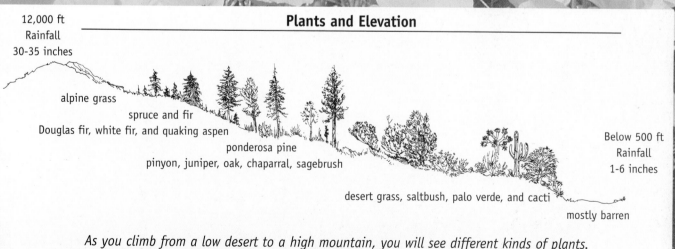

Plants and Elevation

12,000 ft
Rainfall
30-35 inches

alpine grass

spruce and fir

Douglas fir, white fir, and quaking aspen

ponderosa pine

pinyon, juniper, oak, chaparral, sagebrush

Below 500 ft
Rainfall
1-6 inches

desert grass, saltbush, palo verde, and cacti

mostly barren

As you climb from a low desert to a high mountain, you will see different kinds of plants. The temperature gets cooler as you climb. There is more rain at higher elevations, too. Which plants can live without much water? Which plants need cooler air and more water?

ANIMALS IN ARIZONA

Arizona has many kinds of *habitats*, or places where animals live. Black bears, mountain lions, elk, deer, javelina (HAV-vah-lee-ah), and antelope make their homes here. Buffalo and sheep live here, too.

Beavers like colder climates, but they can live in any stream lined with aspen or cottonwood trees. They build dams and ponds along the San Pedro River.

Long ears give mule deer their name. They eat leaves and shrubs. They live in both mountain forests and desert country.
Photo by Lindsey Pehrson

A beaver chews on a log.
Photo by Lynn Chamberlain

Mountain lions are also called cougars. They eat deer and other animals.

Coyotes live everywhere in Arizona. They sleep in the shade by day and come out at night to look for food. They eat rabbits and other small animals. They will also eat insects, plants, and garbage. They sometimes kill calves and sheep.

The Loyal Burro

Long ago, burros carried supplies for men who were looking for gold. But then burros became wild. They took over land near the Grand Canyon. The burros ate grass that other animals needed to survive. They drove away thirsty animals from waterholes.

Today, the government has an "adopt a burro" program. This program protects burros. Burros are good pack animals that can carry heavy loads. They are good guard animals. Many ranchers use burros to protect their sheep and cattle. Burros attack coyotes by kicking them with their sharp hooves. Burros also make good pets. Burros are a living symbol of the Old West. Yee-aw-yee-aw!

Discovering Arizona

Birds

Many kinds of birds live in Arizona. Do you know the names of any birds where you live?

Arizona's smallest bird is the hummingbird. The largest is the wild turkey. The turkey lives in pine forests.

Desert doves and quails also live in Arizona. The "coo kuk coo coooah" sound of the dove is pleasant to hear. It is fun to see a mother quail dashing along a trail with her chicks.

The cactus wren is our state bird. It makes its nest in the touch-me-not cholla cactus. How do you think the cactus got its name?

The roadrunner has long legs, a long tail, and a long neck. It can run almost twenty miles per hour. Unlike most birds, it will eat snakes and lizards.

Have you ever watched a turkey vulture on a hot summer day? This large bird glides smoothly in the air. It does not flap its wings very much. When you see vultures circling, you know there's something to eat below.

The cactus wren is our state bird.
Photo by Richard Cummins

Hungry Hummingbirds

Hummingbirds eat more than twice as much as they weigh each day. You would have to eat more than 150 pounds of **nectar** and insects every day to eat as much as a hummingbird does! Nectar is the sweet liquid from flowers. They need a lot of nectar so they have enough energy. Hummingbirds use a lot of energy flapping their wings more than fifty times each second!

Sharp-Eyed Hawks

A hawk can see very well. It can spot a rabbit running on the ground two miles away. If a hawk could read, it could perch on a football goalpost and read this book hanging from the other goalpost.

The red-tailed hawk is the most common large hawk in Arizona. Take a drive in the country. You might see one perched on a telephone post or soaring overhead.

Fish

There are many kinds of fish in our lakes and streams. Bass, catfish, bluegill, trout, pike, and others make fishermen happy. Arizona's state fish, the Apache trout, was named for the Fort Apache Reservation where it is found.

Reptiles

Reptiles are animals such as snakes, lizards, and turtles. Reptiles are cold-blooded. That means their body temperature is the same as the temperature around them.

Reptiles can survive in the desert because they stay in the shade or go underground during the heat of the day. They hunt food in the coolness of the early morning or at night. This makes them hard to find if you go looking for them.

A desert tortoise moves very slowly.
Photo by Lynn Chamberlain

During the cold months, reptiles *hibernate.* This means they crawl into a cave or hole and sleep all winter. Their hearts beat slowly. Their breathing almost stops.

Reptiles lay eggs. When the eggs hatch, tiny baby reptiles start new lives. Rattlesnakes, however, do not lay eggs. They give birth to live snakes.

For scientists who study reptiles, Arizona is a good place to work. There are nearly 100 kinds of reptiles in the state. About half of these are snakes.

Snakes

Most snakes in Arizona are harmless. Only rattlesnakes and the coral snake are *poisonous.* That means they can make people really sick if they bite them. Look out for rattlesnakes. In a split second, one can strike.

The coral snake is small. It has black, red, and yellow bands on its body. People don't see this snake very often.

Rattlesnakes are found in many parts of Arizona.

Lizards

Many kinds of lizards are found in the deserts and mountains of Arizona. The lizards are very good at living here. Their coloring blends into the landscape. Most of them have clawed toes. The toes help them run on the loose sand and climb rocks.

Discovering Arizona

Lizards eat bugs, spiders, and other insects. One busy lizard can eat hundreds of insects every day. All lizards are harmless except the Gila monster.

Don't ever pick up a Gila monster! The slow Gila monster is the only poisonous lizard in the United States. It stores fat in its tail for times when food is hard to find.

The chuckwalla lizard hides in a strange way. It races to a crack in a rock. Then it puffs in air and wedges its body tightly in the crack. Native Americans used a stick to poke the lizard's hide and pull it loose. They ate the lizard's meat.

A horned lizard is sometimes called a "horny toad." It has a thin, flat, oval body. It has a circle of scaly horns behind its head that looks like a crown. This lizard hangs out near ant dens, lapping up ants. If scared, it may hiss and squirt blood from its eyes.

Like birds, lizards of many kinds give a sense of motion to the quiet desert. They streak across the sands or along a backyard fence. When frightened, they dash off.

The Gila monster is the only poisonous lizard in the United States. The adult male is about a foot long. It minds its own business if left alone, but if you try to touch it, it may bite!
Photo by Lynn Chamberlain

A chuckwalla hides in rock cracks and puffs its body up with air.
Photo by Lynn Chamberlain

Lesson 3

Memory Master

1. What is Arizona's main tree used for timber?
2. What is a habitat?
3. What types of reptiles live in Arizona?

Beautiful Arizona

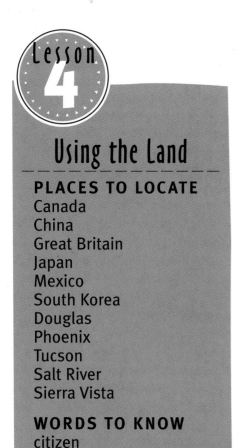

Lesson 4

Using the Land

PLACES TO LOCATE
Canada
China
Great Britain
Japan
Mexico
South Korea
Douglas
Phoenix
Tucson
Salt River
Sierra Vista

WORDS TO KNOW
citizen
dam
reservoir

USING AND CHANGING THE LAND

All over the world, people use and change the natural land. The land provides water, food, wood, and minerals the people need.

In Arizona, we raise crops and animals on the land. We cut timber for wood to build houses. We make bricks out of clay from the earth. We dig ditches to bring water to farms. We build *dams* across rivers. Dams are huge walls across rivers that hold back water.

Dams and Reservoirs

Everyone needs water. They need to drink and cook with it, wash with it, and water their crops with it. Machines in dams use rushing water to make electricity.

Native Americans and pioneers built homes near rivers and lakes. Then the small towns grew and grew, until there were so many people they needed more water. The people had to find a way to change their natural environment.

You will read about the Hohokam people in another chapter. They were the first to make dams and dig canals to bring water from rivers to their farms.

Modern people have also changed their environment by building dams. By opening and closing parts of the dam, workers control the amount of water that passes through. This stops raging rivers from flooding.

Water backs up behind the dam and fills in whole valleys. The new lake is called a *reservoir*. Canals from the reservoir take water to farms and cities. People also boat and fish in the reservoirs. The lakes made by humans are popular places in dry Arizona.

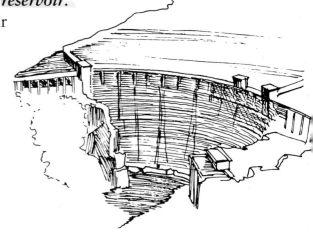

Glen Canyon Dam

Hoover Dam

Parker Dam

Roosevelt Dam

Coolidge Dam

THE IMPORTANCE OF WATER

"Where water flows, Arizona grows!" This saying is very true in the desert. People in Phoenix get much of their water from reservoirs along the Salt River. But two-thirds of Arizona has to use water pumped from under the ground.

Tucson pumps most of its water out of the ground, but not enough rain seeps into the ground to replace all the water being used. Tucson could run out of water someday.

Farmers pump a lot of groundwater to water cotton and other crops. This makes the ground sink. Here and there a big crack appears in the earth.

The Central Arizona Project helps solve water problems in the desert. Big pumps take water out of the Colorado River. Canals brings the water to the Salt River Valley. Another canal takes part of the water to Tucson.

Have you ever seen the falls on the Salt River?
Photo by Willard Clay

Many tourists visit the Grand Canyon each year.

SHARING GOODS AND INFORMATION

People travel from place to place. Arizona has good roads. People ride in cars, trucks, trains, and airplanes. Sky Harbor in Phoenix is a busy airport.

Products made in Arizona's factories, mines, and farms are shipped all over the world. Mexico, Canada, Great Britain, Japan, South Korea, China, and other countries buy our products. We also buy things from other countries.

More and more people are moving to Arizona to live and work. They come from all parts of the country and the world. They bring new ideas with them. We all learn from each other.

Thousands of tourists visit Arizona each year. Some come for a short vacation. Some come for business. Others come for the winter to enjoy the warm sun.

OUR TIES TO MEXICO

Mexico is right next door to us. People, ideas, and products move back and forth. Mexico sends fresh vegetables, cattle, and other products to Arizona. Some products are made in American factories in Mexico. These factories pay Mexican workers.

Many Mexican visitors shop in Tucson, Sierra Vista, and Douglas. It is common to see signs that say *Se habla español* (Say AH-blah ess-pahn-YOL) in store windows. *Se habla español* means "Spanish is spoken."

Many people from Mexico have become American **citizens.** Spanish radio and TV stations make it easier for Mexican Americans to keep their language and culture. Many Mexican Americans also keep their culture by going back to Mexico to see their families.

What do you think?

Many people don't want American companies to move to Mexico. They say Americans need the jobs. What do you think?

Lesson 4

Memory Master

1. How have dams changed our environment?

2. What does the Central Arizona Project do?

3. Where in the world are Arizona products shipped?

Discovering Arizona

What's the Point?

Millions of years ago, pressure from the earth pushed up the land that is now Arizona. It created mountains and plateaus. Today, there are three main land regions in Arizona. They are the Plateau Region, the Mountain Region, and the Desert Region.

Arizona has many different landforms, climates, plants, and animals. All of these natural features make Arizona beautiful. We also have many human features. People are making more buildings and roads. We also trade products and ideas with people all over the world.

What will the future be like? Having enough water may be our biggest problem. Many people think about ways to save water. One student said, "I will sing shorter songs in the shower." What can you do?

Activity

The Ways We Use Water

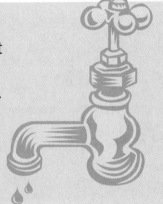

1. With your classmates, make a list of twenty ways water is used. Your list might include things like drinking, cooking, cleaning, and swimming.

2. Pretend there is not enough water. You have to take five things off your list. What can you live without?

3. Pretend things just got worse. You must cross off five more uses of water. What are the most important things left on your list?

Activity

Dams in the Desert

Rivers are important in Arizona. So are the dams that have been built on them. Choose one of the dams in Arizona and do some research on it. Find out why it was built. How many years did it take to build? How do people use the lakes that formed behind the dam?

Geography Tie-In

Your Region

You have read about Arizona's three land regions. What region do you live in? Do some research on your region. What are some of its natural and human features? What makes your region different from Arizona's other regions?

Chapter 3

"In the soft hours of early evening one can almost hear the footsteps of the Old Ones as they climb ladders to their homes in the canyon walls. You can almost hear the children's laughter as they chase the wind."

—Sandra Stemmler in Children of the Old Ones

Timeline of Events

These dates are about when scientists think the people lived here.

9500 B.C.E.*
The first people come to Arizona.

1000 B.C.E.
The Archaic People start to grow corn.

| 10,000 B.C.E. | 8,000 B.C.E. | | 1,000 B.C.E. | | 0 | C.E.* 200 |

8000 B.C.E.
The Archaic People live in Arizona.

*B.C.E. = Before Common Era
*C.E. = Common Era

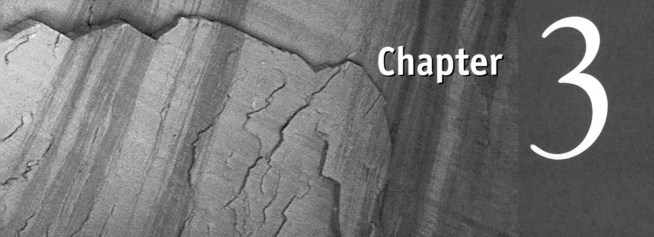

Chapter 3

The First People of Arizona

The Anasazi built this ancient cliff house in Canyon de Chelley. Today it is known as the White House Ruins.

Photo by Kindra Clineff

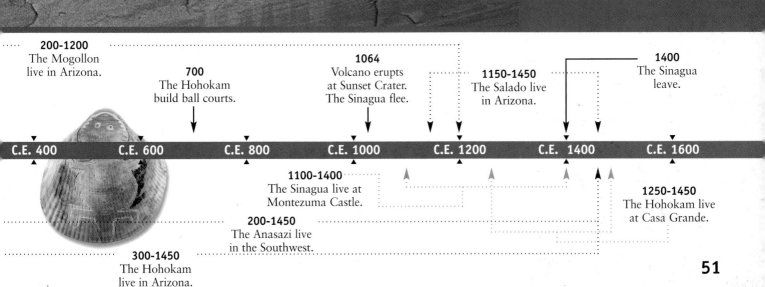

200-1200
The Mogollon live in Arizona.

700
The Hohokam build ball courts.

1064
Volcano erupts at Sunset Crater. The Sinagua flee.

1150-1450
The Salado live in Arizona.

1400
The Sinagua leave.

C.E. 400   C.E. 600   C.E. 800   C.E. 1000   C.E. 1200   C.E. 1400   C.E. 1600

1100-1400
The Sinagua live at Montezuma Castle.

200-1450
The Anasazi live in the Southwest.

1250-1450
The Hohokam live at Casa Grande.

300-1450
The Hohokam live in Arizona.

51

Prehistoric People

PEOPLE TO KNOW
Archaic People

WORDS TO KNOW
archaeologist
archaic
artifact
atlatl
awl
hunters and gatherers
native
prehistoric

What do you think?

Do we always know how people who lived thousands of years ago used an item? For example, a deer made out of twigs might be a child's toy. It also might be a craft people liked to make for fun. Or it might be something much more important.

Why do you think it is hard for scientists to figure out how people lived in the past?

THE FIRST PEOPLE

Native Americans were the first people to live in America. *Native* means the first people to live in a place. Native Americans have lived in Arizona for more than 11,000 years! They are often called Indians or American Indians.

The early Native Americans did not use words to write down their history. We call them *prehistoric* people. Prehistoric means the time before history was written down.

Learning about Early People

How do we know about the first people who lived in Arizona? The men, women, and children of long ago threw things away. They also dropped things. They left things behind when they moved. We call things that people made and left behind *artifacts*. Artifacts are things like tools, jewelry, baskets, and pots.

Archaeologists are scientists who study clues to learn about people who lived long ago. Many of these clues are artifacts found in the ground. For thousands of years, wind blew dirt over ancient homes and villages and buried them.

Archaeologists uncover artifacts under the ground. They keep careful records as they dig. They start by using string to mark off sections of the ground. They give each section a number. They also number each thing they find so they will know where it came from.

ELEPHANT HUNTERS

The first people in the Southwest were *hunters and gatherers.* They came here looking for food. They found animals to hunt. They also found wild berries, nuts, and seeds to eat. The people were always on the move, looking for food.

Arizona was wetter and cooler than it is today. Thick grass fed many animals. The mammoth was the largest animal. The mammoth looked something like an early elephant.

Mammoth Hunt!

Groups of hunters quietly waited for mammoths or giant bison where the animals came to drink water. The men crept up to the huge animals and thrust in long spears with sharp stone points. After the hunt, the men ate some of the meat. Then they dried the rest in the sun and carried it back to camp. Their families had meat for a long time. They also used the fur for warm robes.

Archaeologists have found two prehistoric hunting sites in southern Arizona. At one site, they found eight spear points in the bones of one mammoth. The other site had bones from nine mammoths, a small horse, a bison, and a tapir.

ARCHAIC PEOPLE

After many years, the climate slowly warmed up. Mammoths and other giant animals became extinct. The people who lived after the elephant hunters are called Archaic People. *Archaic* means very old.

Archaic People moved from place to place. They hunted smaller, faster animals, such as deer. The people also fished in streams and lakes and searched for berries, roots, nuts, and seeds.

Learning to Grow Corn

Later, the people learned to grow corn. They ground corn and wild seeds into flour. They held a stone called a *mano* in their hand. They used it to grind seeds and nuts on a larger stone called a *metate*.

Because the people grew some of their food, they could stay in one place longer. They did not have to move as much in search of food.

The mano and metate were used to grind corn and seeds into flour.

The people learned how to use the roots, stems, flowers, and leaves from plants.

Tools

The people made tools and weapons. They carved sharp edges on spear points. They sharpened stones to use as scrapers to clean the fur off animal skins. They carved animal bones to make fish hooks, needles, and awls. *Awls* were used to punch holes into animal hides so the pieces could be laced together to make clothes.

Later, the people made a spear thrower called an *atlatl*. It was a flat, smooth piece of wood about two feet long with two rawhide loop handles at one end. A long spear was placed in the atlatl. When the hunter threw, the spear flew forward, but the atlatl stayed in his hand. With the atlatl, hunters could throw faster and farther.

Hunters used a spear thrower called an atlatl.

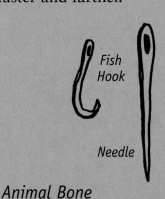

Fish Hook

Needle

Bone Pin

Awl or Punch

Animal Bone Tools

Spear

Lesson 1

Memory Master

1. What scientists study artifacts left by people who lived long ago?
2. What weapon did the people use to kill mammoths?
3. Archaic People learned to grow _____.
4. What tool helped hunters throw spears faster?

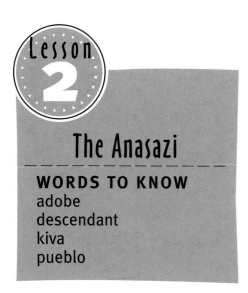

Lesson 2

The Anasazi

WORDS TO KNOW
adobe
descendant
kiva
pueblo

Prehistoric Indian groups in the Southwest traded goods and ideas with each other. They traded turquoise and cotton. They also traded with other Indian groups. They got seashells from the Pacific Ocean and buffalo hides from the plains.

Which prehistoric Indian groups lived closest to where you live today?

LIVING IN ONE PLACE

Farming changed people's lives. For the first time, people could live in one place. They learned to live and work together.

People no longer needed to spend all of their time looking for food. They grew more food than they needed. They saved grain to eat later. People had time to make pottery and play games.

Different groups of Native Americans settled in each of the land regions in Arizona. Look at the map to see where the different groups lived.

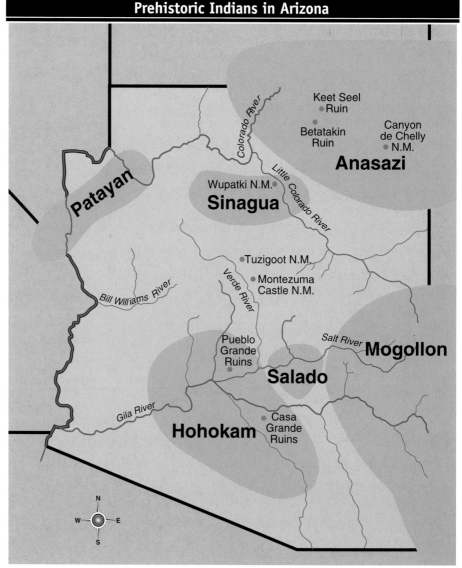

Prehistoric Indians in Arizona

Discovering Arizona

THE ANASAZI

A group of people we now call the Anasazi (ahn-ah-SAH-zee) moved into the plateau region of the Southwest. Anasazi means "the ancient ones." The first Anasazi hunted wild animals and gathered fruits, seeds, and nuts for food. They used an atlatl to throw spears. Over many years, they started using stone daggers as weapons. Even later, the people learned to use bows and arrows.

After hundreds of years, the people started farming and raising animals. They planted corn and beans. The corn was not like our corn. The corncobs were more like a thin shaft of wheat. As time went on, they developed better corn. They even had popcorn. They raised turkeys. They had dogs to help them pull heavy loads.

Baskets and Pottery

The first Anasazi are called "basketmakers." They wove strong beautiful baskets from part of the yucca plant or wet willows that bent easily. They carried food and water in their baskets. They even put hot stones and water in baskets to cook food.

Hundreds of years later, the Anasazi started making pottery for cooking and storing things. Most of the pottery was black and white, but they decorated some pottery with other colors. They traded pottery with other groups of people for gems, jewelry, copper bells, buttons, and beads.

Clothes

The Anasazi made clothes by weaving yucca fibers, turkey feathers, and rabbit fur together to make robes and skirts. Later groups grew cotton and used it to make clothes.

Anasazi pots were used for storing and cooking food.

Music

In the evenings and for special ceremonies, music could be heard. Archaeologists have found rattles made from deer hooves, whistles from bird bones, and carved flutes.

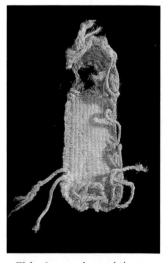

This Anasazi sandal was made from yucca fibers.

From Pit Houses to Cliff Dwellings

At first, the Anasazi built round pit houses partly underground. The sides and roof were made of wood poles covered with brush and mud. A fire burned inside in the winter, and the smoke escaped from a hole in the roof. Since there were no windows, the homes were quiet and dark inside. The people did most of their work and cooking outside in the sun.

Later, groups built large *pueblos*. They were like large apartment houses made of stone or *adobe* bricks. Adobe is made by mixing mud and straw and baking the bricks in the sun. For each roof, heavy logs were laid across the walls. Many of the rooms were used for storing food. The people climbed up wood ladders to go from one level to the next.

Cliff houses were amazing places high up on the sides of rock cliffs. The cliff houses were not easily attacked by enemies. Each day, the people climbed up and down wooden ladders to work in the flat gardens at the top of the mesa or in the valley below.

Each pueblo or cliff house had a round, underground room called a *kiva*. Men climbed down a ladder through a hole in the roof to get inside. They used this room for religious ceremonies.

Keet Seel once had 350 rooms. The name means "broken pottery." Many pieces of pottery have been found there.
Photo by Tom Till

Discovering Arizona

Where Did the Anasazi Go?

No one knows what happened to the Anasazi, but after many years they left their cliff houses. There was a long dry period, and the people needed rain to grow crops. Maybe they moved to find water and never came back.

Many Hopi people living today may be *descendants* of the Anasazi, who returned to that part of the plateau many years later.

What the Trees Tell Us

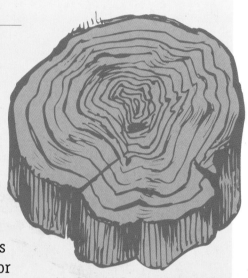

About 100 years ago, Andrew Douglas studied tree rings in Flagstaff. He wondered if trees could tell a story about the weather they had lived through.

Douglas knew that a tree adds a new ring each year. A wet year produces a wide ring. A dry year produces a thin ring.

Douglas studied tree stumps. On paper, he drew a pattern of tree rings for a young tree. He did the same thing with older trees. He made a chart that went back 2,000 years. From studying the rings, he could tell that there was a long drought at the time the Anasazi left.

Douglas helped archaeologists figure out how old some artifacts are. He matched the rings on logs that prehistoric people used for building with the tree rings on his chart. Then he could tell when the trees used by the Anasazi had been alive.

A scientist can figure out how old a tree is by studying its rings.

What do you think

Douglas said that tree rings could tell what happened in the past better than people could. What things could the rings tell? What things about people's lives could not be told by the rings?

Lesson 2

Memory Master

1. How did farming change people's lives?
2. How did the Anasazi use baskets and pottery?
3. Describe life in a cliff house.
4. How do tree rings help us learn about the past?

The Mogollon

PLACES TO LOCATE
Mogollon Mountains
Mexico

WORDS TO KNOW
geometric

MOUNTAIN DWELLERS

The Mogollon (MUH-gee-own) lived in the mountain region. The Mogollon Mountains are named for the Indians who lived there. Like the Anasazi, they hunted animals that were plentiful in the mountains, gathered food from wild plants, and grew corn. The mountains had a lot of wild berries and nuts, so the people didn't grow as much of their food as the Anasazi did. They grew corn, dried it in the sun, and ground it into flour. They ate what they needed and stored the rest for winter.

Houses

Families lived together in a village of pit houses on the side of a mountain that got the most rain. Like the Anasazi, the people later built pueblos and cliff houses of stone and adobe. They used kivas for special ceremonies. They may have learned how to build these houses from visiting with the Anasazi. The adobe homes had thick walls that kept the homes warm in the winter and cool in the summer. The adobe was so sturdy that parts of the homes can still be seen today.

The people traded ideas and things they made with other groups of Indians. They got many ideas from the Anasazi. They may have learned about cotton from the Hohokam.

An archaeologist carefully sweeps the dirt off a pot at an ancient Mogollon pueblo.

Discovering Arizona

Pottery

Today, Mogollon pottery is famous for the pictures of animals, people, and *geometric* designs of triangles and other shapes. The designs are black on a white background. Pictures on Mogollon pottery help us see what their lives were like. Men are shown picking bugs off of corn plants. Other people are setting traps to catch birds. Some are killing deer with a bow and arrow. Others are dancing.

The people sometimes buried pottery with a person who died. A hole was punched in each pot before it was put in the grave, because the Mogollon believed that each pot held the spirit of its owner. The spirit was freed from the pot through the hole.

A plate made by Mogollon people shows a man spearing a very large fish. The size of the fish on the plate shows that fish were important to the people.

Where Did the Mogollon Go?

No one knows why the Mogollon left their mountain villages. Some mixed with other Indians, especially the Anasazi. Archaeologists believe that many Mogollon people went to Mexico. No Native Americans in Arizona today are descendants of the Mogollon.

Lesson 3

Memory Master

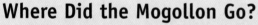

1. Where in Arizona did the Mogollon live?
2. Describe how the people got food.
3. Compare the Mogollon and Anasazi homes.
4. What designs and pictures did the people paint on pottery?

The First People of Arizona

Hohokam

PLACES TO LOCATE
Snaketown
Salt River

WORDS TO KNOW
ancestor
etch
irrigate
pitch

THE HOHOKAM

The Hohokam (HO-ho-kahm) were the first *irrigation* farmers in the Southwest. They did not rely only on rain to water their crops. Instead, they dug canals and brought water from rivers. They grew cotton, corn, beans, and squash.

Workers built a dirt or rock dam across a river. The water rose higher and higher behind the dam until it formed a small lake.

Workers dug canals with stone and wooden tools. They carried dirt away in baskets. They dug many miles of canals. The water flowed into the canals from the Gila and Salt Rivers. The canals carried water to the corn and cotton fields.

Cactus for Dinner

The Hohokam ate many different plants. One was the prickly pear cactus. People took off the poky needles and baked the cactus in pits. Then it was ready to eat. People also ate deer, lizards, mice, squirrels, turtles, and rabbits.

Villages

The largest Hohokam village was at Snaketown. Most of the people there lived in pit houses. A family dug a pit in the ground. Then they built the frame out of logs. They covered the frame with brush and mud. The house was cool in summer and warm in winter. Some of the houses were small, and some were large.

The Hohokam later built large pueblos. Many families lived there. One large pueblo was Casa Grande (KAH-sah GRAHN-day). It is a national monument now. *Casa Grande* means "big house." Pueblo Grande is another example.

Pueblo Grande
• Snaketown
Casa Grande

Casa Grande was built on the top of a high earth mound. It was four stories high. It could have been home to a chief or priest, or it could have been a place to view the stars. Today, a roof has been built to shelter the ancient walls of Casa Grande.

The First People of Arizona

Arts and Crafts

The Hohokam made beautiful jars, bowls, and pots. They also wove cotton into cloth. They made clay figures. They carved jewelry out of bone. They traded with other tribes to get seashells and other items to use in their artwork.

The Hohokam learned to *etch*. They drew a design on a shell with *pitch*. Pitch is the sticky sap of a pine tree. The design was usually of an animal such as a toad. Then they soaked the shell in acid made from a cactus fruit. The part of the shell not covered with pitch was eaten away by the acid to show the design.

A person etched a turtle on this shell. The Hohokam got shells from other Indian groups that lived near the ocean.

Hohokam pottery has beautiful designs. Some of this pottery was found at Snaketown.

Archaeologists think the Hohokam played ball. They dug a large, flat court below ground level. Players tried to get a leather ball through one of the rings on the sides of the court. Players could use only their elbows, knees, and hips to move the ball.

Where Did the Hohokam Go?

Hohokam means "those who have vanished." No one knows why the Hohokam left their villages. Their farmland may have been flooded, or irrigating may have made the soil too salty to grow crops. Maybe a great flood ruined their dams and canals. Maybe they left because of disease or war.

The Hohokam probably stayed somewhere in the desert region. Many archaeologists believe that the Hohokam are **ancestors** of the modern Pima (PEE-mah) and Tohono O'odham (TO-hone-oh AH-ah-tom) tribes. An ancestor is a family member who lived a long time ago.

Lesson 4

Memory Master

1. How did building canals help the Hohokam?

2. What did the Hohokam eat?

3. The Hohokam may be the ancestors of what modern Indian groups?

The First People of Arizona

THE SINAGUA

The Sinagua lived near today's town of Flagstaff. The word *Sinagua* (seen-AH-gwah) means "without water." The people depended on rain, not canals, to water their crops.

Volcano Erupts

For many years, the Sinagua farmed in peace. Then a nearby volcano erupted. Hot lava flowed across the land for miles. Smoke and ash filled the sky. The people were scared. They fled from their homes. Today, the volcano is called Sunset Crater. It has never erupted again.

The Sinagua moved back after a while. They found that the volcanic ash had made their soil rich. The news spread, and some Anasazi and Hohokam moved in.

Houses

The style of Sinagua houses changed. Before the eruption, the people lived in pit houses. They used logs to build the frame of the house. They covered the logs with grass or bark and earth.

The Sinagua lived at Wupatki for a while.

66

After the eruption, the Sinagua built stone pueblos with flat roofs. This pueblo style house can be seen at Wupatki (woo-PAHT-kee) National Monument today.

After many years, there was a long period when there was little rain. The Sinagua had to move again. Many of them went to the Verde Valley. They learned to irrigate their fields. The people built more stone pueblos there. They built a large pueblo called *Tuzigoot* (TOO-zi-goot). At one time, 200 people lived at Tuzigoot. It was a busy place.

Wupatki •

• Tuzigoot

The First People of Arizona

67

Montezuma Castle

Photo by Willard Clay

The Sinagua built a cliff house over the Verde River. Today we call it Montezuma Castle. It was misnamed for Emperor Montezuma, the last ruler of the Aztec Indians in Mexico. The first American settlers chose that name because they thought the Aztecs had built the great cliff dwelling.

Montezuma Castle was like an apartment house. It had thick stone walls. It had five floors. The floors were separated by huge logs. To get the logs, the people cut down trees from a nearby forest with stone axes. The people carried the logs on wooden ladders up the 100-foot wall to the cliff house.

Door openings were small, so that rooms were warmer in the winter. Also, an enemy had to bend over and enter headfirst. People inside could knock the person down before he could harm them.

Today, you can visit this cliff dwelling. If you do, think about what life was like for the children your age who lived there many years ago.

Everyday Life

Hunters killed deer, antelope, rabbits, and ducks for meat. They used salt to make their food taste better and last longer without spoiling.

People ground corn, wove cloth from cotton, dried animal skins, and made baskets. They made jewelry out of shells, turquoise, or a red stone. They made stone axes, knives, and hammers.

The Sinagua traded some of these things with other groups of people. They got parrots from Mexico and pottery from the Anasazi. The Sinagua never made their own pottery.

Where Did the Sinagua Go?

The Sinagua suddenly left, but no one knows why. Was there not enough rain? Did other tribes attack the peaceful Sinagua? Did disease kill the people?

Whatever their reasons for leaving, the Sinagua likely went north to Hopi country. Today, the Hopi have a story about some people joining them from the south.

THE PATAYAN

The word *Patayan* (Pa-TIE-in) means "ancient ones." Today they are also known as the Hakataya. Long ago, they farmed along the banks of rivers. During flood seasons, they went to the desert to hunt animals and to gather plants. After a flood, they returned to raise crops in the rich soil.

Patayan villages were washed downriver long ago, but archaeologists have found some artifacts. The people made gray-brown pottery and shell jewelry. They tied tree trunks together to build houses.

Some modern Native American groups are the descendants of the Patayan. They are the Cocopah, Maricopa, Mohave, Hualapai, Yavapai, and Havasupai tribes. You will learn more about these tribes in the next chapter.

The people planted corn, beans, squash, and pumpkins on the flat ground above or below their cliff houses.

THE SALADO

The Salado (sahl-AH-doh) lived near the Anasazi, Hohokam, and Mogollon, so their cultures were much the same. They irrigated corn, beans, squash, and pumpkins. The farmers carried food and water to their cliff houses. You can see the houses today at Tonto (THAN-toe) National Monument and at Besh-ba-Gowah in Globe.

Lesson 5

Memory Master

1. What does the Spanish word *Sinagua* mean?
2. What is our name for the last volcano to erupt in Arizona?
3. What natural materials did the Sinagua and Salado use to build their homes?

What's the Point?

The land was clean. Clear water flowed in the rivers. Wild horses, bison, camels, and mammoths roamed the land. For thousands of years, hunters and gatherers wandered over what is now Arizona. Just surviving was hard. Sometimes there was not enough rain to grow food. Sometimes there was too much rain and there were floods.

Life changed when people learned to farm and dig canals. For the first time, they could live in one place. They no longer spent all of their time searching for food. Many built large pueblos and cliff houses. After hundreds of years, some of the groups left and never returned.

Activity

Bury a Time Capsule

Would you like someone in the future to find things you've left behind? What could they learn about your lifestyle?

1. Collect things that describe what your life is like now. Your class picture, a ticket stub from a sporting event or movie, a newspaper, a coin, and an empty box of your favorite cereal are all good things to put in a time capsule. You could even make a tape of your favorite songs.

2. Put everything into a waterproof container with a tight lid. Glass and plastic work well. Label the container with the date. Decorate it for fun.

3. Bury your time capsule in your yard for people to find in the future.

Geography Tie-In

A Hunter

Thousands of years ago, a hunter kneels by a campfire in Arizona. He uses his spear to draw a river on the ground. He points at a bend in the river. He says, "Big animals will come to drink the water here. They will come south for the winter. We will eat well!"

1. How does the hunter know that the animals will come south for the winter?

2. How will this help the people to eat well?

3. Write a short story or draw picture of the hunter.

Primary and Secondary Sources

What helps you learn about people of the past? Books? Movies? Photographs? How about spears, pottery, or even bones?

There are two kinds of sources to help us learn what happened a long time ago. We have primary sources and secondary sources. What is the difference?

Primary sources are made by the people who were there at the time. Primary means "first," or a first-hand account. A spear point is a primary source. A piece of mammoth bone is a primary source. Can you think of others?

Secondary sources are made or written later about things that happened in the past. A book about the Anasazi is a secondary source because the author didn't actually see that little boy practice throwing a spear. The author didn't see the family sleeping peacefully at night around their campfire because it was too long ago.

On a piece of paper, number from 1 to 10. Put a "P" for primary source, or an "S" for secondary source by each item.

1. A movie showing a mammoth hunt

2. A model of Montezuma Castle

3. A stone knife found in an ancient cliff house

4. A mano and metate found by an archaeologist

5. A book about the early Native Americans

6. A painting of a Hohokam child

7. A drawing of a pit house

8. A piece of Mogollon pottery

9. Pottery found at Casa Grande

10. A Sinagua necklace

Chapter 4

"Beauty will come in the dawn and beauty will come with the sunlight. Beauty will come to us from everywhere, where the heaven ends, where the sky ends. Beauty will surround us. We walk in beauty."

—Billy Yellow, Navajo

Native Americans in Arizona

These sheep live on the Navajo Reservation in Monument Valley. A long time ago, herding sheep became the Navajo way of life. Families walked out over the high plateaus with their flocks of sheep. They used the wool of the sheep to make yarn, which they dyed and wove into beautiful rugs and blankets. They made delicious stew with the meat.

Photo by Tom Till

Native Americans in Arizona

PEOPLE TO KNOW
Athapascan Tribes
  Apache
  Navajo
Pueblo Indians
  Hopi
Desert Farming People
  Cocopah
  Maricopa
  Mohave
  Pima
  Tohono O'odham
  Yaqui
  Yuma
Plateau Tribes
  Havasupai
  Hualapai
  Paiute
  Yavapai

WORDS TO KNOW
mesa
reservation
warrior

NATIVE AMERICANS IN ARIZONA

Arizona's history is rich with the lives of Native Americans. They have lived here for a very long time. Each group has its own language, land, and special way of living life.

Today, more Native Americans live in Arizona than in any other state. They live in cities and towns. Many also live on lands called *reservations.* These lands have been set aside for them by the government of the United States.

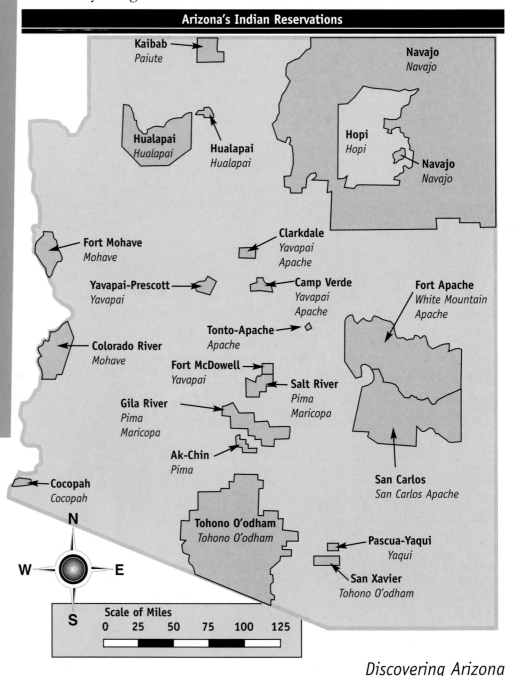

Arizona's Indian Reservations

Kaibab
Paiute

Navajo
Navajo

Hualapai
Hualapai

Hualapai
Hualapai

Hopi
Hopi

Navajo
Navajo

Fort Mohave
Mohave

Clarkdale
Yavapai Apache

Fort Apache
White Mountain Apache

Yavapai-Prescott
Yavapai

Camp Verde
Yavapai Apache

Colorado River
Mohave

Tonto-Apache
Apache

Fort McDowell
Yavapai

Salt River
Pima Maricopa

Gila River
Pima Maricopa

Ak-Chin
Pima

San Carlos
San Carlos Apache

Cocopah
Cocopah

Tohono O'odham
Tohono O'odham

Pascua-Yaqui
Yaqui

San Xavier
Tohono O'odham

N
W   E
S

Scale of Miles
0   25   50   75   100   125

74

Discovering Arizona

FOUR MAJOR CULTURAL GROUPS

Native Americans in Arizona can be divided into four major groups. Each group has a common history and lifestyle.

• **Athapascan Tribes:** The Athapascan (ath-ah-BASS-kan) tribes include the Navajo (NAHV-ah-hoh) and the Apache (ah-PATCH-ee). At different times of the year, they moved to places where they knew there would be fresh water and plants for their animals. They visited the same places year after year. They were also *warriors*. They fought with other groups for rights to their land.

• **Pueblo Indians:** The only Pueblo Indians now in Arizona are the Hopi (HOE-pee). Their ancestors have lived on the same *mesas* for over 1,000 years. A mesa is a hill with a flat top. It is smaller than a plateau. It was easy for the Hopi to protect their homes, because it was hard for enemies to hide when they had to climb to the top of the mesas to attack.

• **Desert Farming People:** Water is important to the desert farming people. The Colorado and Gila Rivers have helped the people survive.

The Pima (PEE-mah), Tohono O'odham (TOE-hone-oh AH-ah-tom), Yaqui (YAH-kee), Cocopah (KO-ko-pah), Maricopa (mair-ih-KOH-pah), Mohave (mo-HAHV-ee), and Yuma (YOO-mah)are often thought of as part of this group, too, but they look different and have a different culture.

• **Plateau Tribes:** The Havasupai (have-ah-SOO-pie), Hualapai (WALL-ah-pie), Paiute (PIE-oot), and Yavapai (YAV-ah-pie) live in northern Arizona. Most of the plateau tribes used to be hunters and gatherers. Only the Havasupai were farmers.

Boys share the comics on a Sunday afternoon. They live on the Navajo Reservation.

Lesson 1

Memory Master

1. What is a reservation?
2. What reservation is closest to where you live?
3. What are the four main Native American groups in Arizona?

Athapascan Tribes

PEOPLE TO KNOW
Apaches
Navajos

PLACES TO LOCATE
Canada

WORDS TO KNOW
chant
clan
hogan
nation
sacred
silversmith
wickiup

NAVAJO

The Navajo call themselves *Dineh*. This word means "the people." They came from Canada hundreds of years ago. The Navajo became sheepherders and spread out over the country with their flocks of sheep.

The Navajo are one of the biggest Native American groups in the United States. They are the biggest tribe in Arizona. They are called the Navajo Nation. A ***nation*** is a very large group of people with the same language, beliefs, and government. The Navajo Nation elects their own government leaders.

Schools

Navajo children learn to speak and write both Navajo and English at school. They are also taught the beliefs of their people. They are taught to live in harmony with the earth and with other people.

Navajo children practice their writing in 1950.

Navajo Nation Zoo

The Navajo Nation has the only "tribal zoo" in America. The zoo is home to birds that are hurt and need help. It is also home to bears, elk, deer, coyotes, sheep, bobcats, skunks, fish, and snakes. These animals can be found in the wild on the Navajo Reservation.

Would you like to watch a porcupine eat an ear of corn?

You can see many wild animals at the Navajo Nation Zoo.

Discovering Arizona

Hogans

The Navajo sheepherders lived in **hogans.** Hogan means "home." The hogan walls had to form a circle. They could have eight to twelve sides if they were made of logs. All hogan doors faced east to greet the morning sun.

Some people still live in hogans today. Some hogans have glass windows and are made of stone. Many Navajo also live in modern homes.

Hogans were made of mud, logs, or stone.

Many Navajo children live in modern houses.

"You use what is on your land. If you have lots of mud, you make a mud hogan. If you live close to rocks, you have a stone one, and if you live close to logs, then you have a wood one. Most of the time, people will use a mixture of rock, log, and mud."

—Darrel Begay, Navajo

What do you think

In this picture, there is a modern power plant and a Navajo sheepherder.
How does this picture show that two different worlds have met?

Native Americans in Arizona

77

Family

Family is very important to the Navajo. A man must marry a woman from a different *clan*. When a baby is born, he or she becomes part of the mother's clan. A clan is made up of families who have the same ancestors. A clan name is like a last name. Examples of clan names are Feather People, Blue Bird People, Mud Clan, Many Hogans Clan, and Red Streak Clan.

Humor is important to the Navajo people. When a child laughs out loud for the first time, the family has a celebration.

Arts and Crafts

Some Navajo women weave blankets and rugs. They use the wool from the sheep they raise. They spin thread from the wool. They color thread with dyes made from roots, berries, plants, and soil.

Some people are good *silversmiths*. They make silver crosses, buttons, belts, necklaces, and other jewelry. They use turquoise and other stones in the jewelry.

Work

Like other people in Arizona, the Navajo are ranchers, policemen, government workers, miners, factory workers, and teachers. They run restaurants, auto repair shops, and gas stations. Some families on the reservation help tourists. Others still raise sheep like their ancestors did a long time ago.

This Navajo girl is learning to weave.
Photo by LaVelle Morris

78

Discovering Arizona

The Navajo often wear beautiful jewelry made of silver and turquoise.

Native Americans in Arizona

A SPIRITUAL PEOPLE

The Navajo believe the earth is *sacred,* or holy, and should be respected. They want to live in harmony with the earth and other people. Navajo people look for beauty all around them.

Dances are important to the Navajo. The dances keep people in harmony with nature and the gods. Some dances are held to cure sickness. People sometimes dance at night around a bonfire. One of their dances is called the Fire Dance. This dance is done to protect the Navajo from fires that could hurt their land.

Navajo Singers

The Navajo use *chants* to honor their gods. Chants are special songs or words. They are like prayers. There are chants to cure sickness, to bless a new home, and to keep dangers away. Sometimes people chant to music.

Navajo men called singers speak chants. A singer is a holy man. He is sometimes called a medicine man because he helps people feel better when they are sick.

A Navajo sand painter shows people how a sand painting is made and then erased.

Singers make sand paintings as they chant. The Navajo word for sand painting means "place where the gods come and go." A singer makes sand paintings on the dirt. The singer colors sand with ground rocks, flowers, and wood. He uses the sand to draw pictures of sacred people and symbols.

When the sand painting is done, the singer wipes it off the dirt ground. The Navajo believe that sand paintings have special powers and the gods would be upset if they did not destroy the paintings. They don't want people to steal the painting's special powers.

Today, Navajo make some sand paintings to be kept. You might see them in museums or shops.

APACHE

The Apache are cousins of the Navajo. The Apache also came from Canada many many years ago, but the two groups split after they got to the Southwest. The Apache settled in the mountains. They divided into groups made up of related families. Each group had a chief and headwoman.

The group did not stay in one spot for long. They roamed from place to place. When they did stay in one place, they lived in *wickiups.* These were huts made of poles covered with grass or brush. The top was shaped like a dome. Like the Navajo hogans, the door of the wickiup faced east. Today, the Apache live in modern homes instead of wickiups.

The Apache were said to be kind and gentle to their families, but they could be cruel to their enemies. The Apache used bows and arrows. Later, they used guns.

Apache warriors knew how to hide themselves. They tied brush to their heads. They rubbed dirt on their bodies. Sometimes they crawled on the ground in order to sneak up on their enemies.

Long ago, the Apache lived in small wickiups made of brush. They gave some shade from the desert sun.

Apaches were fierce warriors. These men posed for a picture in a photographer's studio.

Two Groups

Today, Arizona is home to two Apache groups. They are the San Carlos and the White Mountain Apache.

Many San Carlos Apache work for the government. Some work in copper mines or on cattle ranches. Some have jobs as fire fighters. Some make jewelry from a green gemstone called peridot.

The White Mountain Apache make money from logging and cattle ranching. Many also work for the Fort Apache Timber Company.

Tourists visit the Fort Apache Reservation. There are trout streams, lakes, and forests on the reservation. Ski slopes are popular in the winter.

Apache Rodeo and Fair

A fun event on both of the Apache reservations is the rodeo and fair that is held every year. Apache cowboys compete for prizes. People perform dances, and there is plenty of good food.

A girl parades at the White Mountain Apache tribal fair.
Photo by Stephen Trimble

Young Apache girls take part in a traditional ceremony.
Photo by Stephen Trimble

Lesson 2

Memory Master

1. What is the Navajo Nation?
2. Name three things you learned about the Navajo.
3. Name three things you learned about the Apache.

Discovering Arizona

HOPI

The Hopi still live on the same land as their ancestors, the Anasazi. The Hopi village called Old Oraibi (Oh-RYE-vee) is one of the oldest villages in the United States. It is on the top of a high mesa in the desert.

The name Hopi means "peaceful people." But the Hopi have not always been at peace. In fact, they built their villages high on the mesas for protection from other Indians and from people who later came to Arizona.

The Hopi make beautiful pottery, baskets, and silver jewelry.

Pueblo Indians

PEOPLE TO KNOW
Anasazi
Hopi

WORDS TO KNOW
kachina

These Hopi children are catching fish.
Photo by Stephen Trimble

HOPI RELIGION

The Hopi hold many religious ceremonies. Some parts of the ceremonies are held in underground kivas. Other parts are held in the village plazas.

The Snake Dance is a sacred rain dance. Priests hold live snakes in their mouths and dance. The priests talk to the snakes. "Go back to the gods," they say. "Tell them the Hopi are good and need rain."

"It is dancing day. All the people are very happy. They have brought some corn and watermelons for the children. In the afternoon there is a big rain storm. Everybody gets wet, the kachina also. The water is running all over the fields. So we are very glad."

—*Crow-Wing, Hopi*

Kachinas

Kachinas are important to the Hopi. A kachina is a god or spirit who lives in the spirit world. There are hundreds of kachinas. There are sun kachinas, rattlesnake kachinas, and clown kachinas.

A kachina dancer wears a mask, chants, and shakes a rattle made from a turtle shell. The dancer tells the kachina spirit the people's needs. The dancers give gifts like candy and dolls to children.

Kachina dolls represent spirits.

What do you think

Can you think of problems that Native Americans who grew up on a reservation might have if they moved to a city? What problems would people who live in a city have if they moved to a reservation?

Lesson **3**

Memory Master

1. What is the name of the oldest Hopi village?
2. Why did the Hopi build their villages on mesas?
3. What is a kachina?

Discovering Arizona

PIMA

The Pima can trace their ancestry back to the Hohokam. They called themselves *Akimel O'odham*. This name means "river people."

The Pima have lived near the desert rivers for hundreds of years. They grew corn. They grew cotton to make cloth. They also hunted and gathered wild plants. They later grew wheat and raised sheep and chickens.

Today, the Pima live on three reservations in Arizona and in other towns.

This Pima girl has a big smile.
Photo by Stephen Trimble

TOHONO O'ODHAM

The Tohono O'odham are related to the Pima. Long ago, they moved to the desert. *Tohono O'odham* means "Desert People." Their old name *Papago* means "Bean People." The first Tohono O'odham farmed in the summer. They built dams to hold back rainwater. They used the water to irrigate their fields of beans, squash, and corn.

Tohono O'odham people harvest fruit from the saguaro cactus.

Lesson 4

Desert Farming People

PEOPLE TO KNOW
Cocopah
Maricopa
Mohave
Pima
Tohono O'odham
Yaqui
Yuma

WORDS TO KNOW
astronomy

"As long as we had water here, we had plenty of things to eat. Instead of having telephones, the chief of the village would get up on his house and holler early in the morning, 'We're going to build dams and get ready for the water!'"

—*Archie Russell, Pima*

Living on the Reservation

The Tohono O'odham Reservation is very large, but much of the land is not good for farming. It is not easy to grow crops in the desert. The Tohono O'odham still gather wild desert foods. In the summer, they harvest the fruit of the saguaro cactus. They cook the fruit, then pour off the thick syrup. They use the syrup to make jam or wine. They grind the seeds into flour.

The Tohono O'odham also raise cattle. They have many cattle. In dry years, hundreds of cattle die because they can't find enough to eat. Many people work part of the year in towns and cities close to the reservation.

Tohono O'odham Fair and Rodeo

The All-Indian Tribal Fair and Rodeo is the biggest event on the reservation. There are dances, games, and a Miss Tohono O'odham contest.

Visitors come to the fair to shop for baskets. The Tohono O'odham make coiled baskets in many shapes. They use yucca fiber, beargrass, devil's claw, and willow to make the baskets.

The Kitt Peak National Observatory

The Kitt Peak National Observatory is on the Tohono O'odham Reservation. It is an astronomy research center. **Astronomy** is the study of the stars and planets. Why do you think some Tohono O'odham say the scientists at Kitt Peak have "long eyes"?

Scientists can see craters on the moon with powerful telescopes.

Kitt Peak was built on the top of a mountain.

Discovering Arizona

MARICOPA

The Maricopa live on the Gila and Salt River Reservations with the Pima. Long ago, unfriendly tribes drove them away from the Colorado River.

The Maricopa are famous for their pottery. They used to use different pots for different things. Women used to carry large water pots on their heads. The people used a pot for syrup.

Today, Maricopa people earn money by farming and growing cotton. They also work at jobs in Phoenix.

YAQUI AND COCOPAH

Both the Yaqui and Cocopah came from Mexico. Some of their people still live in Mexico. The Cocopah people farmed near the Colorado River many years ago. They gathered grass seeds for food and fished in the river. Today, the river does not run through their land because people have built dams upstream. The dams control how much water flows in the rivers.

The Yaqui celebrate the Easter holiday and have their own "Easter Ceremony." They live on the Pascua Yaqui Reservation.

MOHAVE AND YUMA

Long ago, the Mohave lived near the Colorado River. The mesquite tree provided them with food. They used its bark to make shoes and its sap to make glue. Today, the Mohave grow a lot of cotton, alfalfa, melons, and lettuce.

The Yuma also lived near the Colorado River. They were warriors and farmers. Today, they still depend on the Colorado River for water.

Lesson 4

Memory Master

1. Who are the Pima's ancestors?
2. What was the old name of the Tohono O'odham?
3. For what craft are the Maricopa famous?

Ida Redbird
1892–1971

Ida Redbird was a Maricopa woman who made beautiful pottery. She grew up on the Gila River Reservation. When she was a young girl, her mother taught her how to make pottery. When she was older, she taught other people how to make pottery.

Redbird had a special way to make pottery. She first tasted the clay to see if it was salty. If it was too salty, the salt would make the pots look white when they were done. After she had good clay, she pounded it into powder. Then she added water and mixed it like bread dough. She used a curved wood paddle and stone to shape her pot. She baked the pot in a hot fire. Sometimes she used tree sap to paint designs on the pots.

Native Americans in Arizona

Plateau Tribes

PEOPLE TO KNOW
Havasupai
Hualapai
Paiute
Yavapai

HAVASUPAI

The name *Havasupai* means "People of the Blue-Green Waters." The Havasupai have lived at the bottom of the Grand Canyon for many years. They were protected from invaders because their villages were not easy to get to.

Today, people can get to their reservation by an eight-mile long trail or by helicopter. There are beautiful waterfalls and pools of water here. The rock walls give a sense of protection. People from all over come to visit this beautiful land. Some Havasupai make money from tourism.

The Havasupai live at the bottom of the Grand Canyon.

HUALAPAI

The Hualapai live near the Grand Canyon. They used to spend a lot of time gathering food and hunting. They gathered fruits, berries, and nuts, and hunted antelope, sheep, and rabbits. They moved around a lot so that they could find food.

Today, the Hualapai raise cattle, sell timber, and make money from tourism. They take care of the only road that goes into the Grand Canyon. They have their own policemen, firemen, and leaders.

PAIUTE

The Paiute had to be creative in finding food. They ate seeds and roots. They also ate deer, antelope, and lizards. They learned how to make cone-shaped baskets to carry food. They also made basket cradles for babies.

Today, they farm and raise cattle on the Kaibab Reservation. Many people are also involved in tourism and the tribal government.

YAVAPAI

Long ago, the Yavapai had to move around a lot to find food. They learned to make beautiful baskets.

Today, the Yavapai live on reservations at Camp Verde and Fort McDowell. The Verde River runs through their land. During the summer, people like to cool off by the river. Children float down the river in inner tubes. Many of the people work in or near Prescott.

Lesson 5

Memory Master

1. Which group lives at the bottom of the Grand Canyon?
2. Which group lives on the Kaibab Reservation?
3. How did Carlos Montezuma help Native Americans?

ARIZONA PORTRAIT

Carlos Montezuma
1867–1923

Carlos Montezuma was a Yavapai Indian. As a small child, he survived a battle between two Indian groups. His mother died, and he was separated from his father. The woman who took care of him after the battle sold him to a photographer for $30. The photographer thought he would be a good model. He gave him the name Carlos Montezuma.

Montezuma went to school and became a doctor. Later, he came back to live on the Salt River Reservation. His message to the people who came to see him was simple. He said, "Learn and make something of yourself." He spent a lot of time helping Native Americans win their rights.

What's the Point?

Native Americans are a very important part of Arizona's history. They were the first people to live here. There are four major groups of Native Americans in Arizona. Each group has several tribes with a special history and culture.

Today, some Native Americans live on reservations. Other Native Americans live in cities and towns. Native Americans work to preserve their traditions, culture, and language.

Activity

Write about Native Americans

Choose a Native American group that lives in Arizona today. Use library books, encyclopedias, and the Internet to find information about the group.

After you have done your research, write a report about the people's history and culture. Share your report with your class.

Geography Tie-In

Think about how Native Americans built their homes in the past. What natural resources did they use? How do we build homes today? How are the ways alike? How are they different?

Sand Painting

You have read about Navajo sand painting ceremonies. They are important to the Navajo people, and they are sacred. The sand paintings show symbols that are special to the Navajo.

You can create your own type of sand painting. You will need:

- A piece of cardboard or wood
- Glue
- Colored sand

Choose a symbol that is important to you. It could be a symbol for your family, for nature, for your home, or for anything that you like.

On a piece of cardboard or wood, trace the symbol that you have chosen. Draw a design inside the image that you traced. Apply a thin layer of glue on one section of the design at a time. Use your finger to lightly cover each part of the design with colored sand.

Carefully complete the sand painting, and let the glue dry. You can show your painting to your class or your family. Tell them about Navajo sand painting. Make sure you mention that the Navajo don't use glue for their paintings. They make their designs on the floor and then sweep them away after their ceremony is done.

Native Americans in Arizona

"The myths and legends of golden cities and fabulous wealth in the New World ran rampant throughout the Old. Any story was believable as long as it reflected riches."

—Marshall Trimble

Timeline of Events

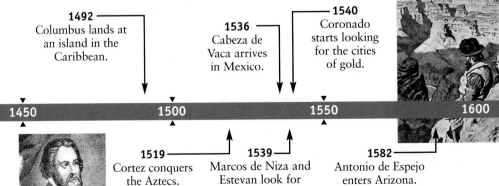

1492 — Columbus lands at an island in the Caribbean.

1536 — Cabeza de Vaca arrives in Mexico.

1540 — Coronado starts looking for the cities of gold.

1450   1500   1550   1600

1519 — Cortez conquers the Aztecs.

1539 — Marcos de Niza and Estevan look for the cities of gold.

1582 — Antonio de Espejo enters Arizona.

92

Chapter 5

Spanish Explorers and Missionaries

Spanish priests and Indian workers built the San Xavier del Bac mission near Tucson over 200 years ago. It was a place for the Indians to learn about the Catholic religion.

Photo by Richard Cummins

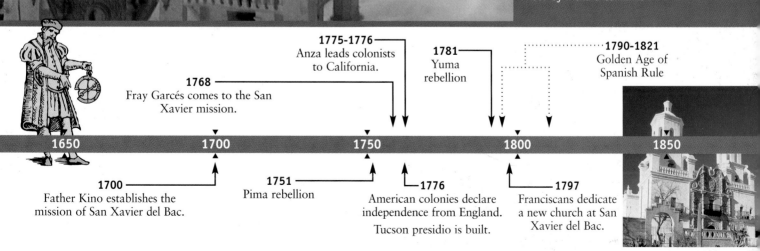

1768 — Fray Garcés comes to the San Xavier mission.

1775-1776 — Anza leads colonists to California.

1781 — Yuma rebellion

1790-1821 — Golden Age of Spanish Rule

1650   1700   1750   1800   1850

1700 — Father Kino establishes the mission of San Xavier del Bac.

1751 — Pima rebellion

1776 — American colonies declare independence from England.
Tucson presidio is built.

1797 — Franciscans dedicate a new church at San Xavier del Bac.

The New World

PEOPLE TO KNOW
the Aztecs
Christopher Columbus
Hernán Cortés
Estevan
Montezuma
the Taino
Cabeza de Vaca

PLACES TO LOCATE
Asia
China
England
France
the Indies
Spain
Russia
Mexico
Tenochititlán
the Caribbean
Gulf of Mexico

WORDS TO KNOW
conquer
slave

A NEW WORLD

People in Europe had been trading with people in Africa and Asia for many years. Europeans wanted rugs, silk, gems, and spices from those lands.

Traders had to travel a long way to buy goods. The trip to Asia by land was long and dangerous. Explorers wanted to find a shorter route to Asia that would make trade easier and faster.

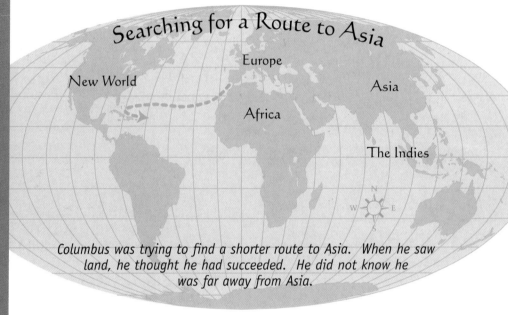

Searching for a Route to Asia

New World — Europe — Asia — Africa — The Indies

Columbus was trying to find a shorter route to Asia. When he saw land, he thought he had succeeded. He did not know he was far away from Asia.

CHRISTOPHER COLUMBUS

Christopher Columbus was an Italian explorer who believed he could reach Asia by sailing west. Many people did not believe Columbus's plan was a good idea. He had to convince the king and queen of Spain that paying for his voyage would be worth their money. He told them he would bring Christianity to the people of Asia, and he would bring back riches for Spain. After Columbus asked many times, the king and queen gave him three ships, a crew, and supplies for the trip.

After about a month at sea, Columbus and his crew arrived at islands in the Caribbean. Columbus called the people on the islands "Indians" because he thought he had reached islands near China called the Indies. Columbus had really met the Taino people. The Taino and other groups had been living there for over two thousand years.

Claiming Land for Spain

Columbus claimed the islands for Spain. Everywhere he went, he met the Taino people. Columbus wrote about the people in his journal. He was impressed by their peaceful ways, but he also thought he was better than them:

> They were well-built, with good bodies and handsome features. . . . They would make fine servants. . . . With fifty men we could make them do whatever we want.

Many of the Taino wore small gold jewelry, which led Columbus to believe that there were gold mines on the islands. What he did not know was that there were only tiny bits of gold in the rivers.

When Columbus went back to Spain, he took native plants, parrots, and six Taino prisoners on his ships.

Gold and Slaves

Back in Spain, Columbus said he had found islands near Asia with "many spices, and great mines of gold and other metals." He told the king and queen that if they paid for a second trip, he would bring them "as much gold as they need . . . and as many **slaves** as they ask." A slave is a person who is viewed as property and forced to work for his or her owner.

This time, the king and queen gave Columbus seventeen ships and a crew of more than twelve hundred men. When Columbus arrived at the islands, he demanded the Taino people provide him with gold. The Spanish killed many of the Taino when they could not give Columbus the gold he wanted. Later Columbus forced 500 Taino into his ships to be sold into slavery in Europe.

Columbus returned to the islands two more times. He still thought he was in Asia, and he never gave up his hope of finding gold.

Many of the Taino died of diseases they caught from European sailors. Many were killed by the Spanish. There were over one million Taino people when Columbus arrived. Thirty years later almost all of the Taino people were dead.

When Columbus landed, he placed a "large holy cross" on the land. He named the island San Salvador, which meant Holy Savior. Whose point of view is shown in this painting? If the Taino people had painted the scene, what would it look like?

What do you think

Columbus did what many other explorers had done. They claimed land for power and riches. Did Columbus have a right to claim land for Spain when the Taino were already living there? What do you think?

EXPLORING THE NEW WORLD

When other European explorers heard about Columbus's voyage, they wanted to go on journeys of their own. They wanted to find gold and riches. Men from Spain, England, France, and Russia sailed to America. They claimed land for their countries even though thousands of Native Americans already lived there. Soon explorers would make it to the land that is now Arizona, and life would change for the native people living there.

How New Was the New World?

Europeans called the land Columbus claimed the "New World." But it was not really new. Thousands of groups of people, like the Taino, had been living there for thousands of years. The land was only new to the Europeans.

CREATION OF NEW SPAIN

A Spanish explorer named Hernán Cortés (air-NAHN kor-TESS) was one man who was excited about the New World. He sailed to Mexico after hearing about a city that was full of gold. He learned of an Aztec ruler named Montezuma who had palaces full of riches. At first, Montezuma invited Cortés into his city. Soon trouble began, and a war started. Cortés took gold and riches for himself from the Aztecs.

In time, Cortés **conquered** the Aztec city and named it Mexico City. Thousands of Aztecs were killed. Like the Taino, many of the Aztec people died of diseases they caught as a result of the Spanish coming to their city.

The Spanish claimed a large piece of land that included present-day Mexico and Arizona. They named the land New Spain.

Cortés shipped boatloads of Mexican gold and silver back to Spain. Many Spanish men were excited about exploring New Spain. They wanted to find gold. They set out on long voyages across the ocean to explore the land Cortés had made famous.

Cortés claimed a large piece of land for Spain in what is now Mexico and Arizona.

CABEZA DE VACA

About twenty years after Cortez, a group of over 500 Spanish explorers sailed in five ships from Spain to the New World. Three of the ships were lost at sea, but the others landed in Florida. Many of the explorers sailed back to Spain. The rest explored the land on foot and horseback, but many got very sick. They had trouble finding food, and the Indians were unfriendly. Fearing for their lives, the men built log boats and tried to sail to Mexico where they knew other Spanish people were living. They used horsehair to tie the logs together.

Along the coast of the Gulf of Mexico, the wind howled and waves crashed against the rafts, washing some of the men into the sea. Others made it to an island near the Texas shore.

Indians made the men their slaves. A slave is someone who is owned by someone else. Most of the men died from lack of food. Cabeza de Vaca, however, won fame as a medicine man. He rattled a gourd and made the sign of the cross. Many of the sick got well, and the Indians brought gifts of deer meat and prickly pear fruit. Because the Indians thought he had special powers, Cabeza de Vaca was given freedom to visit other tribes.

Cabeza de Vaca and three others, including a black slave named Estevan, headed for Mexico. Along the way, they met Indian groups who told them wild stories of the "Seven Cities of Cíbola." They said the cities were made of gold.

The starving men slowly walked through the Southwest. When they finally arrived at a Mexican town, they were happy to be with Spanish people again. It had been eight years since they had left Spain. They told the leaders of Mexico City about their journey. The leaders were surprised to see the men still alive. Mostly, the leaders wanted to hear more about the cities of gold.

Cabeza de Vaca and the other men pretended they were medicine men and could cure sick people.

Memory Master

Lesson 1

1. Why did Columbus want to find a short route to Asia?

2. Why were Spanish men eager to explore the New World?

3. Tell the story of Cabeza de Vaca in your own words.

Lesson

2

Cities of Gold

PEOPLE TO KNOW
García López de Cárdenas
Francisco Coronado
Antonio de Espejo
Estevan
Hopi Indians
Viceroy Mendoza
Fray Marcos de Niza
Juan de Oñate
Pedro de Tovar
Zuñi Indians

PLACES TO LOCATE
Mexico
Mexico City
New Mexico
Grand Canyon
Pacific Ocean
Gulf of California
Colorado River

WORDS TO KNOW
interpreter
ore

THE SEARCH FOR GOLDEN CITIES

Viceroy Mendoza was the leader of New Spain. He wanted to find the Seven Cities of Cíbola. He formed a small group to go and look for them. Fray Marcos de Niza was the leader of the group. He was a Catholic missionary. Estevan was the guide.

After many weeks of traveling through the desert, Estevan and a small group of Indians were sent ahead to find the golden cities. Since he could not read or write, Estevan agreed to send a wood cross back to Fray Marcos as a message. A small cross would mean no golden cities had been found. A large cross would mean riches had been found. The men arrived at a city they thought was full of gold. Estevan sent an Indian runner back to Fray Marcos with a cross as large as a man!

Estevan was a tall black man. In some Indian villages he acted like a medicine man. He shook a gourd filled with pebbles and wore red and white feathers. Bells jangled on his ankles and elbows. Most Indians treated him with awe and respect. Many followed him as he traveled.

This mural is in the Arizona State Capitol Building. Estevan is on the far right, and Fray Marcos is next to him. Do you see Estevan's gourd?

Discovering Arizona

When Estevan got to a Zuñi village, things changed. Angry men shot him with sharp arrows. Indian runners went back to tell Fray Marcos the sad news of Estevan's death.

Fray Marcos returned to Mexico City. He told Viceroy Mendoza that he had climbed to the top of a hill and seen a huge golden city with high buildings and turquoise doors. He said the Indians wore giant pearls, gold beads, and emeralds. Viceroy Mendoza believed Fray Marcos and decided to send other explorers to search for the golden cities.

What do you think

Why do you think Fray Marcos said he had seen a golden city? Did he see sunlight on the mud houses, making them sparkle? Did he want Mendoza to think he was successful? Was he afraid to tell the truth?

Coronado traveled from Mexico into the Southwest. He was searching for gold.

FRANCISCO CORONADO

Viceroy Mendoza chose a young nobleman, Francisco Coronado, to lead another group to look for the Seven Cities. Coronado was only twenty-five years old. This time, Fray Marcos went as a guide. It would be his second trip to the desert.

A Grand Army

Many men were eager to go on the journey to get riches and glory. Before they set off, they paraded in front of Viceroy Mendoza. First in the parade were 225 men on horses. Some wore armor and helmets. Then came more than sixty soldiers. They carried swords, spears, and shields. About 1,000 Indians with weapons were next in line. Indian and black slaves brought up the rear to look after the animals. They herded thousands of cattle, sheep, and goats.

Spanish Explorers and Missionaries

The End of the Rainbow

Coronado took a smaller group of men and traveled ahead of the main group. After many days, they ran out of food. They were half-starved by the time they got to a Zuñi village in what is now New Mexico.

The Spanish were in for quite a shock. Here they were at the end of the rainbow, but there was no pot of gold.

Zuñi warriors met the Spanish at the edge of the town. The Zuñis raised their bows and arrows and yelled threats. They drew lines on the ground with cornmeal and told the Spaniards not to cross the lines.

When Indians tried to kill Coronado's *interpreter*, Coronado ordered an attack. With swords flashing in the sun, they rushed toward the Zuñi. In less than an hour the Zuñi were forced to flee. The hungry Spanish ate all the food that was left in the Zuñi homes. The beans and corn were better than gold.

Later, Coronado met with Zuñi chiefs from other places. They had no gold. Coronado wrote the sad news in a letter to Viceroy Mendoza. Fray Marcos took the letter to Mexico City. He was happy to go. By this time, the men were angry with him because all of his stories of rich cities were not true.

Tovar

Coronado sent two groups of his men to explore Arizona. Pedro de Tovar, with the help of Indian guides, took a small group of men to the Hopi villages.

At first, the Hopi were not friendly. But Tovar was not scared. He attacked the Hopi and forced them to give up.

The Hopi told Tovar about a great river and rich Indians to the west. Tovar hurried back to the Zuñi villages to report the Hopi stories to Coronado.

Cárdenas

Coronado was excited. He sent Captain García López de Cárdenas (KAR-day-nass) to find out if the Hopi were telling the truth. Cárdenas and his men stopped at the Hopi villages.

In today's money, Coronado's journey would cost about two million dollars!

Cárdenas reached the Grand Canyon. He was not interested in natural wonders. He wanted gold.

Hopi guides led the Spanish to the Grand Canyon. They were the first Europeans to see this great wonder of the world. But they did not find any gold, so they returned to the Zuñi villages where Coronado was.

Coronado traveled into what is now Texas and Kansas before he returned to Mexico. He never found gold, but he had learned a lot about the land of the Southwest.

Espejo

About forty years after Coronado, other people explored what is now Arizona. Antonio de Espejo (ess-PAY-hoh) was a rich man who lived in Mexico. He and some Indian guides traveled into Arizona, looking for gold and silver.

The group found some silver *ore* near present-day Jerome. Ore is a rock that has metal in it. Espejo took samples back to Mexico, but the Spanish never came back to develop mines.

Oñate

Juan de Oñate (oh-NYAH-tay) was the governor of New Mexico. He was a rich man who spent his own money to bring settlers to New Mexico.

One very cold winter, Oñate led a group of explorers to Arizona's Hopi villages. The men and horses suffered so much from the cold that Oñate decided to take most of them back to New Mexico. First, he sent a smaller group to look for Espejo's silver mines. They found rich silver ore near today's Prescott, but they never sent miners back to dig the ore.

On another trip, Oñate followed the Colorado River across northern Arizona. He went all the way to the Gulf of California and back. He wanted to find the Pacific Ocean so traders could use a water route to China.

Oñate traveled more in Arizona than any other Spanish explorer. He never mined silver and never made it to the ocean, but he did help other people know more about Arizona.

Tall Tales

Oñate heard some strange stories on his trips. The Mohave Indians told the Spanish about a great lake. They said the people at the lake all wore gold bracelets. There was another story about a rich land of bald men. A fat woman with big feet was their leader.

The Indians told another story about a tribe of one-legged people. One tribe slept in trees and another slept underwater. They also told the Spanish that there were Indians along the Colorado River who lived only on the smell of food.

The Spanish brought horses to the New World. Before the Spanish came, there were no horses here.

What do you think

What if the Spanish explorers had found the gold they were looking for? Would it have been right for them to take it from the Indians? Did the Spanish show respect for the Indian people? Did the Indians respect the Spanish?

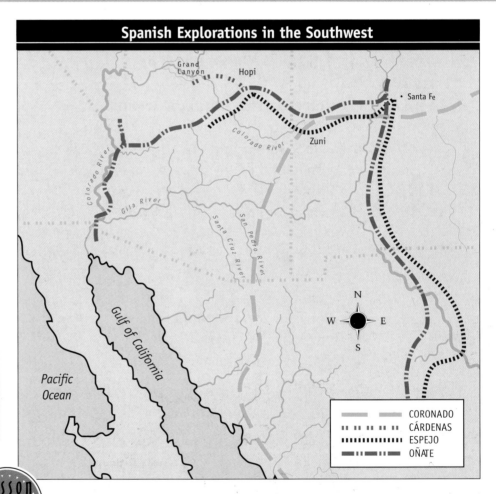

Spanish Explorations in the Southwest

Grand Canyon
Hopi
Santa Fe
Colorado River
Zuni
Colorado River
Gila River
Santa Cruz River
San Pedro River
Gulf of California
Pacific Ocean

N
W E
S

CORONADO
CÁRDENAS
ESPEJO
OÑATE

Lesson 2

Memory Master

1. How did Estevan send back a message to Fray Marcos?

2. Describe the large group that went with Coronado to find the golden cities.

Discovering Arizona

CATHOLIC MISSIONARIES

Gold-seeking explorers hurried through Arizona. They claimed a lot of land for Spain. Catholic priests from Spain traveled with the explorers. The priests mapped the new lands. They wrote about the Native Americans in their diaries.

The priests taught the Native Americans about Jesus. They were *missionaries* who tried to *convert* the Indians to the Catholic religion.

Priests helped Spain claim a lot of land. They became friends with some Indian groups. They could sometimes go where soldiers were not welcome.

Hopis Reject First Spanish Missionaries

There were two groups of Spanish Catholic priests in Arizona—the Jesuits and Franciscans. Jesuit priests came into Arizona from New Mexico, but the Hopi showed no interest at first. Then a priest healed a blind boy. For a while, the Hopi believed the new religion, but then jealous medicine men poisoned the priest. Other priests came to live among the Hopi. The Hopi had their own spiritual beliefs and wanted to live their own way of life.

The Hopi's rejection of the priests affected Arizona's history. It meant that Northern Arizona would not be settled by people from New Mexico, where many Franciscan missions were. Instead, Southern Arizona was settled by priests, soldiers, and other people who came from the south.

Missionaries in Arizona

PEOPLE TO KNOW
Hopi Indians
Pima Indians
Father Kino
Tohono O'odham Indians

PLACES TO LOCATE
Italy
Spain
Washington, D.C.
Pimería Alta

WORDS TO KNOW
convert
mission
missionary

Franciscan priests named the mountains near Flagstaff. They called them the San Francisco Peaks.

Diseases in the New World

When you get a cold, you usually get it from someone else who has a cold. Long ago, the Native Americans got sick from being near the Europeans. They had never had measles or smallpox, so their bodies did not know how to fight off the diseases.

Today, your doctor gives you a shot so you don't get measles or smallpox. You probably already had the shot when you were a baby. But the Native Americans didn't have a shot to protect them from the diseases. Thousands died. In some villages nearly all of the Native American children died.

FATHER KINO

Father Kino is one of the most important men in Arizona history. He was the first successful missionary in the region called the Pimería Alta. He explored this region and made many maps.

Father Kino was born in Italy. In school he studied math, astronomy, and map making. When he was a young man, he got very sick and almost died. After many prayers to help him get well, he wanted to become a priest. He was sent across the ocean to Mexico as a missionary. Then he was sent to Arizona.

Father Kino loved the Indian people. He worked hard, and he was kind and gentle. A priest who worked with Father Kino said, "He never had more than two shirts because he gave everything to the Indians."

Missions

Father Kino set up many *missions.* One mission he set up was at the Indian village of Bac. He named it San Xavier del Bac. Most missions had a simple adobe church with a beautiful carved altar. Indians did the hard work of building the missions. They used wood or saguaro cactus ribs for roof beams. They also used wood for doors, furniture, and for shutters that could be closed over the windows when there was a storm.

Indian families sometimes lived in or near the missions. Father Kino taught the Catholic religion to the Pima and Tohono O'odham. He also taught them new ways to farm. They learned how to plant new grains and fruit trees. They also learned how to raise cattle, sheep, and horses. They rounded up animals in Mexico and brought them to the missions.

An Honored Man

Father Kino died in New Spain. Stories say he died on a bed of two calfskins for a mattress and two Indian blankets for his covers. His saddle was his pillow. Over 250 years later, the people of Arizona honored Father Kino by putting his statue in the capitol building in Washington, DC.

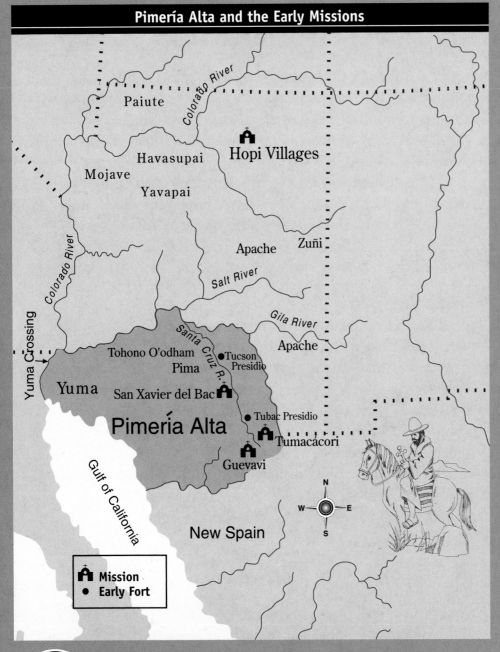

Pimería Alta and the Early Missions

Paiute

Colorado River

Hopi Villages

Havasupai

Mojave

Yavapai

Colorado River

Apache   Zuñi

Salt River

Gila River

Yuma Crossing

Santa Cruz R.

Tohono O'odham   Apache

Pima   •Tucson
                    Presidio

Yuma

San Xavier del Bac

Pimería Alta   • Tubac Presidio

Tumacácori

Guevavi

Gulf of California

New Spain

Mission
Early Fort

Father Kino traveled throughout the Pimería Alta. He helped start twenty-two missions in the region. He spent his life visiting with people at the missions and helping them grow crops and raise livestock.
In his twenty-four years in Arizona, Father Kino traveled over 75,000 miles on his horse. That is one reason why he is called the Padre on Horseback. Padre means father.

Memory Master

Lesson 3

1. What might have been some reasons that the Hopi weren't friendly to the missionaries?

2. Why did the Hopi and other Indians die when they came in contact with the Spanish?

3. List some ways Father Kino helped the Indians.

Lesson
4

After Father Kino

PEOPLE TO KNOW
Apache Indians
Juan Bautista de Anza
Fray Garcés
Pima Indians
Yuma Indians

PLACES TO LOCATE
England
France
Spain
California
New Mexico
Thirteen Colonies
Yuma Crossing
Pimería Alta
Colorado River
Pacific Coast
Gila River

WORDS TO KNOW
colony
independence
presidio
rebel
revolution
route

THE PIMA REBELLION

The Pima Indians were usually peaceful. But long after Father Kino died, they *rebelled* against Spanish rule. The Spanish had forced Indians to work in the silver mines and as servants in homes. They often treated them cruelly. A Pima leader was eager to drive out the Spanish and rule Pimería Alta himself.

The rebellion started at a village south of the present Mexican border. Within a few days, Pima men killed more than 100 miners, cowboys, farmers, and priests. Missions were destroyed, including Kino's San Xavier del Bac. Later, the Pima leader of the rebellion was captured by soldiers near Tucson.

Tubac Presidio

The Spanish wanted to stop more Pima rebellions. They built a *presidio,* or fort, called Tubac. The main job of the soldiers at Tubac was to protect the Spanish soldiers and settlers from the Apaches. Apaches were not river farming people like the Pimas. They were fierce nomadic bands who lived in desert mountains and canyons. Apaches often made hit-and-run raids to drive off livestock.

Fifty Spanish soldiers guarded Tubac. A settlement soon grew up around the fort. The first white woman to come to Arizona came to live with her husband at Tubac.

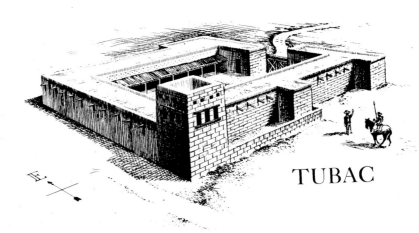

TUBAC

Tubac was built to protect Spanish missionaries and settlers from angry Indians.

106

FRAY GARCÉS

After a time, the king of Spain made all the Jesuit priests leave the New World. However, he let the Franciscans stay in the New World.

The most famous Franciscan priest in Arizona was Fray Garcés (gahr-SAYS). He was born in Spain. When he grew up, he became a priest and was sent to the San Xavier mission.

Garcés liked the Indians, and they liked him. Garcés often visited Pima villages near the Gila River. He learned to speak the Pima language. He took care of the sick during an outbreak of measles. He also baptized many of the Indians. Although he was only thirty years old, the Indians lovingly called him the "Old Man."

"He sits with them in a circle, or at night around the fire, with his legs crossed . . . talking [to the Indians]. . . . And although the foods of the Indians are coarse . . . the father eats them . . . and says they are good for the stomach, and very fine."

—*Fray Pedro Font*

Garcés used a piece of cloth to teach the Indians about Christianity. On one side, there was a picture of the child Jesus. A picture of an unhappy lost soul who did not believe in Jesus was on the other side.

What do you think

Why do you think there were periods of peace and fighting between the Spanish and the Indians? What lessons might we learn about how people treat each other?

The American Revolution

As you have learned, many explorers came to the New World after Columbus. European countries claimed land in North America. Spain claimed Mexico and the Southwest. England claimed the East Coast of North America. England set up thirteen *colonies* there.

After a while, the people in the thirteen colonies became angry. England made them pay taxes that they didn't want to pay. The Americans did not feel like they had a say in their government. They thought they should pay taxes only if they could help make the laws.

The colonists got more and more upset. They wrote a paper called the Declaration of Independence. It said that the colonists had certain rights. It said they had not been treated fairly. It also said they were cutting all ties with England. The colonists named themselves the United States of America. They finally declared their *independence* from England on July 4, 1776. This was the same year that Spain built the Tucson presidio.

A colony is a settlement that is ruled by another country.

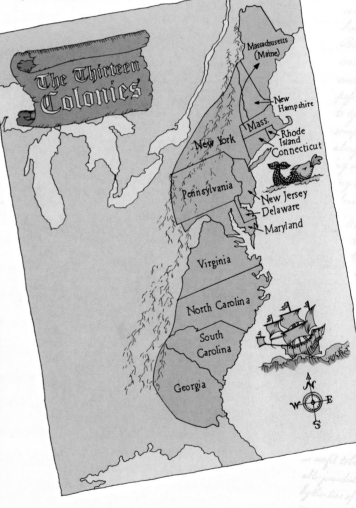

Soldiers said goodbye to their families as they went off to fight in the American Revolution.

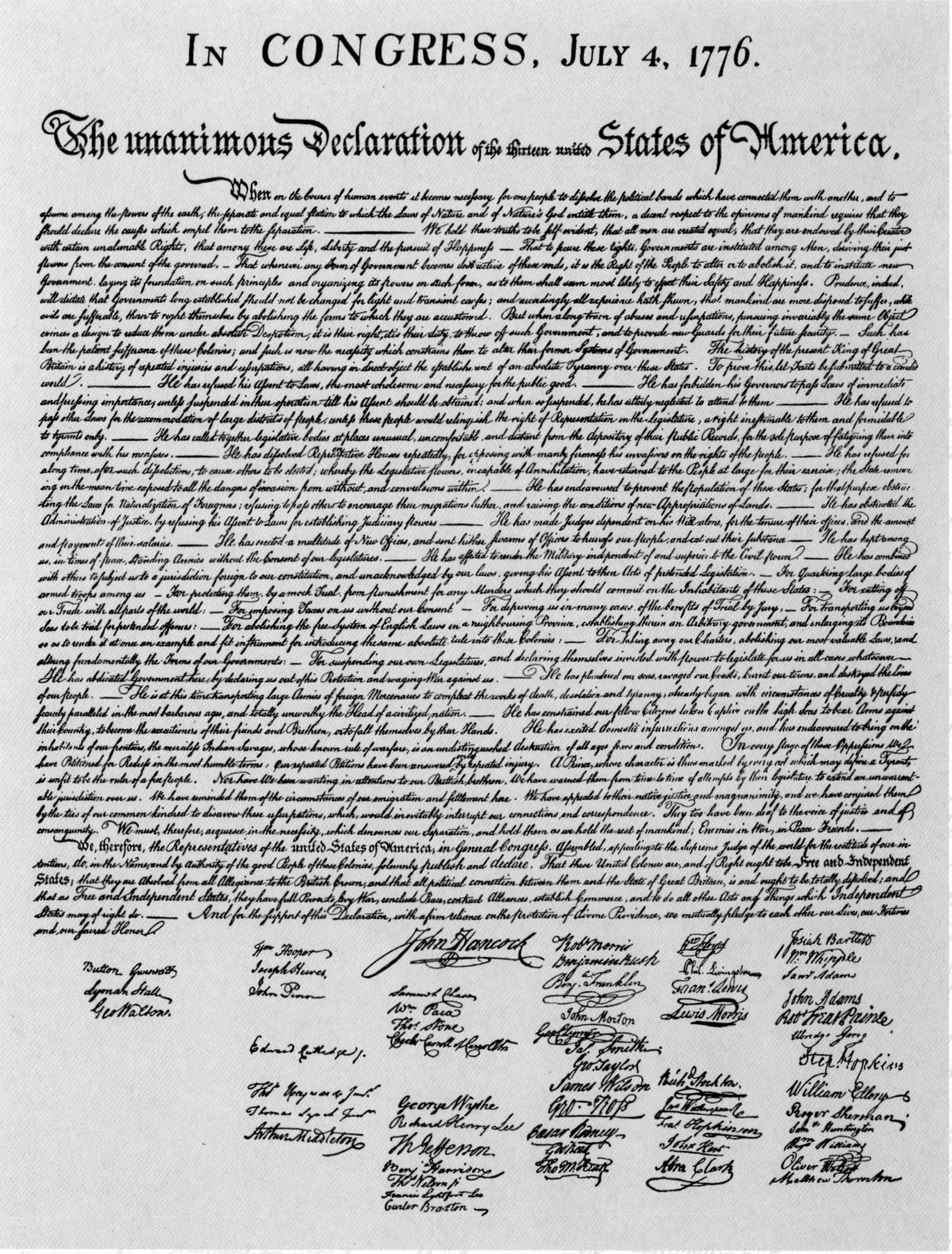

IN CONGRESS, JULY 4, 1776.

The unanimous Declaration of the thirteen united States of America.

In the Declaration of Independence, the colonists said they would no longer be ruled by the English.

Linking the Past to the Present

Do you and your family watch fireworks on the Fourth of July? Most Americans do. They celebrate the day the thirteen colonies declared their independence from England.

Are there any other people in the world fighting for their independence today?

Goodbye to English Rule

Of course, just saying they were free did not bring freedom. The English were angry and didn't want to lose their land. The colonists had to fight a war. The war was called the American Revolution. A ***revolution*** happens when people fight to replace one government with a different government. With the help of the French, the Americans won the war.

ANZA AND GARCÉS

Far away from the thirteen colonies, the Spanish still ruled the Southwest. Juan Bautista de Anza (bau-TEES-tah day AHN-zah) was in charge of the soldiers at Tubac. Anza and Father Garcés planned two trips to California.

Anza wanted to bring settlers to California. But first he needed to find a good way to get there by land. He and a group set off to find a land **route**. They stopped at the Yuma Crossing on the Colorado River. The Yuma Indians gave them watermelon and helped them across the river.

While Anza was busy in California, Garcés explored. He tried to find a good trade route between the Pacific Coast and New Mexico. He was at the Hopi village of Oraibi on July 4, 1776. Do you remember what was happening on that day in the thirteen colonies?

The Hopi did not make Garcés feel welcome. They would not take his gifts of tobacco and shells. At night, he tried to sleep in a dark corner of the village, but he was scared.

I saw [many people coming], the sight of which caused me some fear of losing my life. There came forward four Indians who appeared to be leaders. The tallest of them asked me . . . "For what hast thou come here? Get thee gone without delay back to thy land!"

Anza and his group spent time in Tubac during their journey. They wanted to find a land route to what is now California.

110

THE YUMA REBELLION

At first, the Yuma wanted to be friends with the Spanish. The Spanish set up two settlements at the Yuma Crossing on the Colorado River. Each colony had a mission with two priests. Garcés was one of them. There were also Spanish soldiers and settlers. The Spanish hoped to control the Yuma Crossing because it was the only good place to cross the Colorado River on the way to California.

Some of the soldiers and settlers were not kind to the Yuma. They took the best farmland. They made fun of the Indians, and they crowded the Indians out of the missions. The Spanish fed their horses and cattle mesquite beans that the Indians needed for food.

The Yuma finally rebelled. About fifty Spanish men were killed. All four of the priests, including Garcés, were killed. After the Yuma rebellion, the Spanish stopped trying to control the Yuma Crossing.

This is how early Tucson looked. The wall protected the people from Indian attacks.

Tucson Presidio

After a while, the Spanish moved soldiers from the Tubac presidio to Tucson. The Tucson presidio was well located to defend the San Xavier mission. This fort was the beginning of the city of Tucson.

The San Xavier Mission is sometimes called
the "White Dove of the Desert."
How do you think it got this nickname?

Discovering Arizona

Today, the Tumacácori mission is a national monument.

GOLDEN AGE OF SPANISH RULE

Peace finally came. The Spanish gave up trying to fight the Apaches, and they changed to a peace policy. Spanish officials offered gifts and food to Apaches to stop fighting.

Tucson was growing. More than 1,000 Spanish settlers, soldiers, and Native Americans lived there. Most of the people farmed or raised livestock. Wheat, corn, and beans, were the main crops. The Pima also grew cotton to weave into cloth.

The Spanish opened more mines. Ranchers brought herds of cattle to southern Arizona. The Spanish built more churches. At San Xavier, the Franciscans built a beautiful church. It replaced the mission Kino built that was destroyed in the Pima rebellion. This church is still in use today. At Tumacácori, the Spanish built another large church. The new churches were in the same places as Father Kino's first missions in Arizona.

Lesson
4

Memory Master

1. Why did the Spanish build the Tubac Presidio?
2. Why were the people in the thirteen colonies upset with England?
3. Describe the events at the Yuma Crossing.

Spanish Explorers and Missionaries

What's the Point?

Christopher Columbus' discovery of the New World led to many changes. Explorers from all over Europe were excited and came to explore the land. They claimed it for their countries. Spain claimed Mexico and much of the Southwest.

The Spanish wanted to find gold in the Southwest, but they failed. The cities of gold did not exist. Missionaries came to convert the Indians to Christianity. They set up missions and taught the Native Americans about the Spanish religion and way of life.

Activity

An Important Year

The year 1776 was important. It was the year the thirteen colonies in the East declared their independence from England. It was also the year that Tucson was founded.

Research the lifestyle of the people in the Southwest during this time. What did they wear? What did they eat? What types of housing did they have? How did they get along with other groups of people?

Then research the life of the people in the thirteen colonies during this time. How were the groups different? How were they the same?

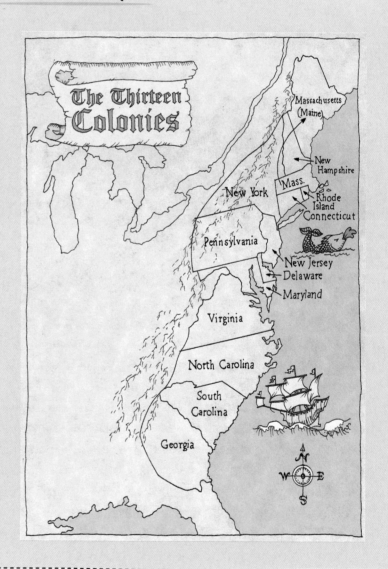

Life at a Mission

The missions in Arizona were churches, schools, workshops, farms, and ranches—all in one. The Native Americans who lived there learned about Christianity, farming, and the Spanish language and way of life.

Two priests were usually in charge of the mission. One priest was in charge of indoor activities. He taught people about religion, led church services, and kept a record of what happened at the mission.

The other priest was in charge of outdoor activities. He taught people how to build buildings, plant and harvest the crops, and raise livestock.

Indian women cooked, washed, and made baskets, soap, and clothes. Children kept animals out of the gardens and did other chores.

Pretend you are a Native American living at a mission. Write a diary entry about what goes on at the mission. Describe how you feel about your life at the mission.

Crops

Indian rooms

Chapel

Cemetery

Geography Tie-In

Spanish Place Names

Make a list of Spanish place names in Arizona. Find Spanish names for Arizona towns, cities, streets, parks, rivers, and lakes. Use a highway map, street map, or phone book to help you create your list.

Chapter 6

"As soon as a child was old enough to toddle, he was thrown on a pony's back, to be held there by a grown person. Among his earliest memories was the rhythm of a horse in motion."

— Jo Moro

Timeline of Events

1821
Mexico wins independence from Spain.

1824
First American fur trappers come to Arizona.

1820 1825 1830 1835

1821
The Mexican government gives huge Arizona land grants to Mexican citizens.

1836
Texas wins its independence from Mexico.

Arizona as Part of Mexico

These children are of Mexican descent. They dressed in traditional Mexican clothes for a special program at school.

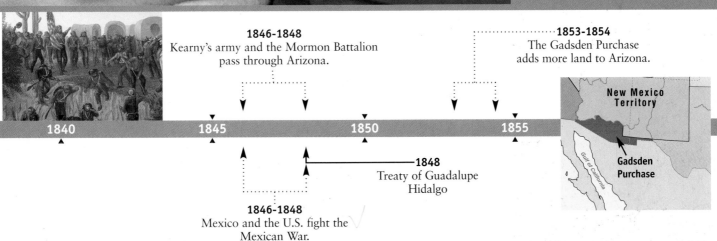

1846-1848
Kearny's army and the Mormon Battalion pass through Arizona.

1853-1854
The Gadsden Purchase adds more land to Arizona.

1840   1845   1850   1855

1848
Treaty of Guadalupe Hidalgo

1846-1848
Mexico and the U.S. fight the Mexican War.

New Mexico Territory

Gulf of California

Gadsden Purchase

117

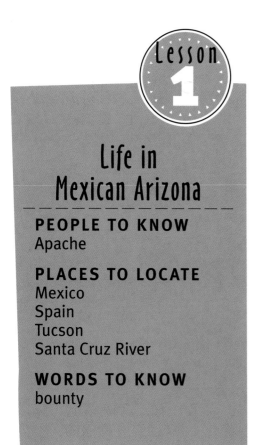
Life in Mexican Arizona

PEOPLE TO KNOW
Apache

PLACES TO LOCATE
Mexico
Spain
Tucson
Santa Cruz River

WORDS TO KNOW
bounty

MEXICAN REVOLUTION

As you know, Mexico and much of the West belonged to Spain. However, like the thirteen colonies, the people in Mexico wanted to rule themselves. Their first revolution failed. But eleven years later, Mexico won its independence from Spain. The land that is now Arizona became part of Mexico.

Mexican soldiers fought for their independence from Spain.

A NEW GOVERNMENT

Life was different after Arizona became part of Mexico. The Mexican government changed some of the ways things were done.

Missions Closed

The new government of Mexico did not think missions were necessary. The new government forced Spanish missionaries to leave. The San Xavier mission did not have a priest for years. At one time, the church and mission buildings were used as barns, horse stables, and as a place for soldiers to sleep. Mexican leaders also sold the Tumacácori mission.

Life in Mexican Tucson

The Mexican government didn't worry much about the people in Tucson since they were so far away. The people had to care for themselves.

People lived in one-room adobe houses. Many were ranchers and farmers. A few hundred friendly Apaches worked for farmers.

People got water from canals near the Santa Cruz River. They gathered desert plants to eat. They made tortillas from flour. Most Tucson homes had a burro flour mill. People ate desert foods, such as mesquite pods and the fruit of the saguaro.

A burro went round and round, turning a stone that ground wheat or other grains into flour.

Mexican Cattle Ranches

People who wanted to move to Arizona and raise cattle got large land grants from the Mexican government. The government gave people a large piece of free land. A rancher could also buy the lands around the ranch for a very low cost. Most of the big ranches were in southern Arizona.

Apache Raids

Spain had given food to the Apache. When Mexico took over, the Apache stopped getting the food. Some Apaches were upset. They attacked Mexican ranches and drove away livestock. Sometimes they carried away women and children. Families who lived on the ranches were afraid.

Almost all the Mexican ranchers left their lands because of the Apache attacks. They left their cattle and moved to towns for safety. Their cattle became wild.

Mexican leaders came up with a plan to stop Apache raids. They decided to give *bounties,* or rewards, for Apache scalps. The scalp-hunters got up to $100 for a head of hair. Sadly, men from the United States and Mexico killed peaceful Mexicans and peaceful Indians as well as many Apaches.

The bounty system made the Apache even angrier. Raids went on for years. Few new settlers came to Arizona.

What do you think

Do you think it was right for Mexican leaders to give a reward for killing the Apache? Could there have been a better way to solve problems between both groups?

Lesson 1

Memory Master

1. From which country did Mexico win its independence?
2. How did land grants help ranches?
3. What are some reasons the Apaches raided ranches?

The Mountain Men

PEOPLE TO KNOW
"Kit" Carson
James Ohio Pattie
Pauline Weaver
"Old Bill" Williams

PLACES TO LOCATE
Europe
Independence, Missouri
Phoenix
Prescott
San Diego, California
Santa Fe Trail
Santa Fe, New Mexico
Scottsdale
Taos, New Mexico
Williams
Yuma
Colorado River
Gulf of California

WORDS TO KNOW
apprentice
flint
pelt
rendezvous
scout

FUR TRAPPERS

Today, Arizona is a growing state with busy cities and many people. It is hard to imagine what this region was like when it was still a wilderness land. Only the bravest and strongest people came to the West. The mountain men were the first Americans to explore Arizona. They helped to open up the West to other American settlers.

The mountain men were also known as fur trappers. They came to Arizona while it was still a part of Mexico. They trapped beavers and other small animals along the rivers. Beaver fur was used to make tall felt hats. This style of hat was popular for men in the eastern United States and in Europe.

Top hats were very popular in Europe.

How to Catch a Beaver

To catch a beaver, a mountain man used a strong steel trap with a long chain. He placed the trap in shallow water. Then he put bait on a twig above the trap. When the animal tried to get the bait, it was caught in the trap and drowned. The trapper took off the fur and dried it. The fur *pelt* weighed up to two pounds. Trappers pressed pelts in bundles and tied them together.

A Mountain Man's Life

Mountain men had to live outside in all kinds of weather. They had to fight off wild animals and keep unfriendly Indians away. However, some mountain men lived with friendly Indians. Some men married Indian women and had children.

Riding their horses, mountain men explored Arizona's mountains, rivers, and streams in search of beavers. They stayed alive in the wilderness by using Indian skills. Some wore buckskin clothes and a fur cap.

Mountain men carried a rifle, gunpowder, a bullet pouch, and a stick used to push the gunpowder down into the rifle. They also had *flints* to start a fire, an axe, a sharp knife, blankets, cooking pots, and traps.

After a season of trapping, mountain men went to the trading post or to a *rendezvous*. There they sold their beaver pelts. They used some of their money to buy flour, salt, coffee, tobacco, and sugar.

Blazing a Trail

After Mexico won its independence from Spain, Americans were welcomed in Santa Fe. It was the closest Mexican town to the United States. Merchants in Santa Fe wanted to exchange their silver, gold, beaver furs, and Indian blankets for American goods.

One man from Missouri put together a huge pack train. He took it 800 miles through Indian country to Santa Fe. He made a lot of money for the goods he brought. Others wanted to make money, too. They used the trail he had made. Fur trappers and mountain men traveled on this trail. It became known as the Santa Fe Trail. It ran between Santa Fe and Independence, Missouri.

The Santa Fe Trail

- - - - Santa Fe Trail

Mountain Men in Our Time

Modern mountain man rendezvous, or meetings, are held all over Arizona each year. Phoenix, Scottsdale, Yuma, Williams, and many other towns and cities hold rendezvous. People dress up as mountain men and camp like the mountain men did years ago. There are lots of things to do and food to eat. There are trading posts where people can buy things mountain men have made.

JAMES OHIO PATTIE

Few mountain men kept a diary. James Ohio Pattie did the next best thing. After his trapping days were over, he wrote a book about his adventures.

Pattie was twenty years old when he came to Santa Fe. He came with his father and a group of traders and trappers. In Santa Fe, he helped rescue a young woman from some Indians. She was the daughter of a man who had been the governor of New Mexico. For his bravery, Pattie won a Mexican trapping license.

Pattie and his father joined a party of trappers. The men were the first Americans to come to Arizona. They trapped along the Gila and Salt Rivers. On one trip, Pattie joined a group of French trappers. Indians attacked the group. Only Pattie and two other men survived.

After a while, Pattie and his father made their last trip to Arizona. When Indians stole their horses, the men made boats out of cottonwood logs. They floated down the Colorado River and hid their furs near the Gulf of California. Then they hiked across the desert to San Diego, California.

The whole group was put in a Mexican jail, where Pattie's father died. Pattie and the other trappers were finally let out of jail. They were let go because Pattie knew a little bit about medicine. The Mexican governor sent Pattie around California to give people shots to keep them from getting smallpox. The disease was killing thousands of settlers and Native Americans.

On the Lookout!

The Mexican government was very suspicious of the mountain men. The government thought the men might steal some of Mexico's land. Mexican soldiers rode through the country, bothering trappers. They often stopped mountain men and took away all of their furs and supplies.

Arizona As Part of Mexico

"OLD BILL" WILLIAMS

A mountain, a stream, and a town in Arizona are named after "Old Bill" Williams. He was a famous mountain man.

Williams began his adult life as a missionary. He worked among the Indians in Missouri, where he married an Indian woman. After his wife's death, he went west over the Santa Fe Trail to hunt and trap.

Williams first came into Arizona with a group of trappers. He was a good trapper. He would show up at Taos with a big bundle of furs. He used the money he earned from the sale of his furs for drinking and gambling.

Williams was over six feet tall. He was thin but tough. He had red hair and a weather-beaten face that had been scarred by smallpox. His walk was strange. He staggered but never seemed to get tired. He could run along streams all day with beaver traps on his back.

Williams had a good shot with the rifle. But he was not able to hold the rifle steady to aim it. He squeezed the trigger just as his rifle swept across the target. Williams was described by a friend as "a dead shot with his rifle, though he always shot with a double wobble, for he never could hold his gun still; yet his ball went always to the spot."

Williams was a good rider. He used short Mexican stirrups that made him lean forward. He rolled up his buckskin pants so that his legs were bare below the knees.

PAULINE WEAVER

Pauline Weaver's mother was an Indian and his father was white. He never went to school and did not know how to read and write.

Weaver trapped up north until he got tired of the cold winters. He decided to come to Arizona. He found plenty of beavers here. He stayed here even though desert beaver furs were not always the best.

Though not a miner, Weaver discovered small pieces of gold along the Colorado and Gila Rivers. He guided a party of gold seekers to a mining area near the Bradshaw Mountains.

"Like the Indian, [Williams] doesn't cook his meat. He is the bravest and most fearless of all."

—*Albert Pike*

Pauline Weaver liked to trap alone.

Weaver was a peacemaker and moved among the Indians without fear. In his older years, Weaver was a *scout* for the army. A scout is sent ahead of a group to gather information about the land and people. When the army assigned Weaver to live at a fort, he refused. He pitched his tent among the willows on the river bottom. That is where he died.

Weaver was the first settler on the site of Prescott. He is called the Father of Prescott. A large, granite rock marks his grave there.

CHRISTOPHER "KIT" CARSON

When Kit Carson was sixteen years old, he became an *apprentice* in a saddle and harness shop in Missouri. He was supposed to learn to make leather goods. He hated working at the shop, so after a year he ran away. He wanted a more exciting life in the West.

While Carson was on his way to Santa Fe, his boss ran an ad in the newspaper. He offered a reward of one cent for Carson's return. This small amount was meant to show that Carson was worthless.

After he got to Santa Fe, the young Carson worked for three years at any job he could get. He learned enough Spanish to work as an interpreter, explaining Spanish words to people who spoke only English.

Carson later joined a group of forty trappers. He trapped the streams of Arizona and California. Carson is more famous as a guide than as a trapper. He traveled all over the Rocky Mountains with explorers.

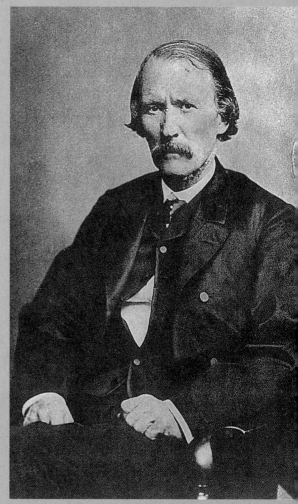

Kit Carson was a famous trapper, guide, and scout.

Lesson 2

Memory Master

1. Why did mountain men come to Arizona?
2. Describe the life of a mountain man.
3. Why was Mexico suspicious of the mountain men?

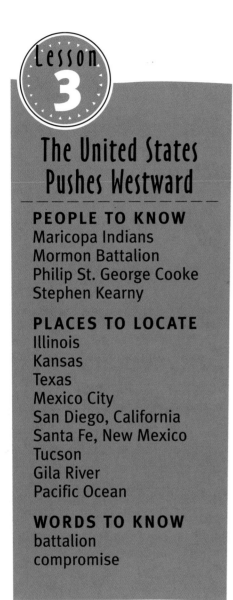

Lesson 3

The United States Pushes Westward

PEOPLE TO KNOW
Maricopa Indians
Mormon Battalion
Philip St. George Cooke
Stephen Kearny

PLACES TO LOCATE
Illinois
Kansas
Texas
Mexico City
San Diego, California
Santa Fe, New Mexico
Tucson
Gila River
Pacific Ocean

WORDS TO KNOW
battalion
compromise

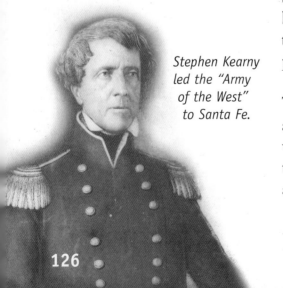

Stephen Kearny led the "Army of the West" to Santa Fe.

THE MEXICAN WAR

Like Arizona, Texas was part of Mexico. Then, Texas won its independence from Mexico and became part of the United States. Mexico was angry about losing Texas, and it still claimed part of the land. Mexico did not accept the new border between the two countries. When Mexican troops crossed the new border into Texas, the United States declared war.

During the Mexican War, U.S. soldiers fought their way to Mexico City. Two army groups crossed Arizona.

The Army of the West

Stephen Kearny led the "Army of the West" across Kansas to the muddy village of Santa Fe. Kearny left most of his army in Santa Fe. He took about 100 soldiers along the Gila River across Arizona. Pack mules carried the group's supplies. At the Pima villages, General Kearny got cornmeal, flour, beans, pumpkins, and melons. Farther downstream, he was able to get cattle from the Maricopa Indians.

The Mexican War was not quite over in California. Mexican soldiers killed many of Kearny's soldiers. Soon after, the Mexican army gave up.

The Mormon Battalion

Leaders of The Church of Jesus Christ of Latter-Day Saints (Mormons) asked their people to volunteer to join a **battalion,** or group of soldiers, to help fight in the Mexican War.

Before the Mexican War, Mormons had been driven out of their homes in Illinois by people who did not like their religious beliefs. The Mormons wanted to prove that they were loyal to the United States, and they needed the money the government paid soldiers.

The Mormon Battalion traveled across southern Arizona. The group fought only one "battle" when they were attacked by a herd of wild bulls. The bulls killed their mules, broke a few wagons, and injured some soldiers. One man wrote in his diary that the bulls were hard to drive off. They "would run off with a half dozen [bullets] in them."

Discovering Arizona

Building a Road

Captain Philip St. George Cooke took charge of the Mormon Battalion in Santa Fe. His orders were to build a road from Santa Fe to San Diego. The United States wanted a good route to California.

In all, the Mormon Battalion made a road over 1,000 miles long. It was called Cooke's Wagon Route. Their road later became known as the Gila Trail. They carried heavy wagon loads over the road through the hot, dry desert, across the wide Colorado River, and through steep mountains.

The Gila Trail was an important route to California. Later, people would travel it on their way to find gold in California. The road would provide a way to get supplies and mail to small and large towns. The Gila Trail helped Arizona and the rest of the Southwest grow.

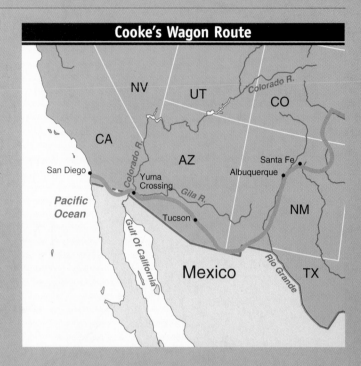

Cooke's Wagon Route

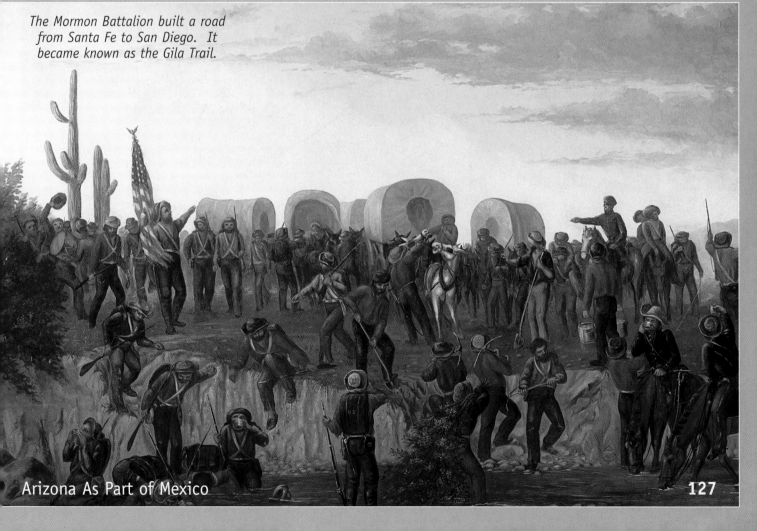

The Mormon Battalion built a road from Santa Fe to San Diego. It became known as the Gila Trail.

TREATY OF GUADALUPE HIDALGO

The Mexican War ended. The United States and Mexico signed a treaty at a small town called Guadalupe Hidalgo. In the treaty, Mexico gave almost half of their country to the United States. The United States paid Mexico $15 million for the land. The land that Mexico gave up was called the Mexican Cession. This was a huge chunk of land in the West, including California, Utah, Nevada, New Mexico and other land. It included most of what is now Arizona.

The Mexican Cession

Mexican Cession

Pacific Ocean

Mexico

The Treaty of Guadalupe Hidalgo gave a huge amount of land called the Mexican Cession to the United States.

The treaty gave Mexico $15 million for the land.

People living in the Mexican Cession could choose either Mexican or U.S. citizenship.

A treaty is an important agreement. When Mexico agreed to the Treaty of Guadalupe Hidalgo, they signed this document and sent it to the United States. Today, the treaty is kept in a safe place.

What do you think

Hilario Gallego amused people with his riddle. He said, "I was born in Mexico, never moved, and lived most of my life in the United States. How could that be?" Can you explain the answer to this riddle?

Discovering Arizona

GADSDEN PURCHASE

A few years later, the United States bought more land from Mexico. A bad map had been used when the Treaty of Guadalupe Hidalgo was signed. The United States said it had not gotten all of the land it should have. The United States wanted more land for a railroad route to the Pacific Ocean.

The United States made five different offers to buy Mexican land. The biggest offer was $50 million for a huge amount of land south of California, Arizona, New Mexico, and Texas.

Mexico, however, was willing to sell only enough land for a railroad route. Mexico would not sell the United States a seaport on the Gulf of California.

After a long debate, a *compromise* was reached. A compromise is a settlement in which both sides agree to give up some of the things they want. The United States agreed to less land. Mexico agreed to sell the land for less money, and it kept its land route to the Pacific Ocean.

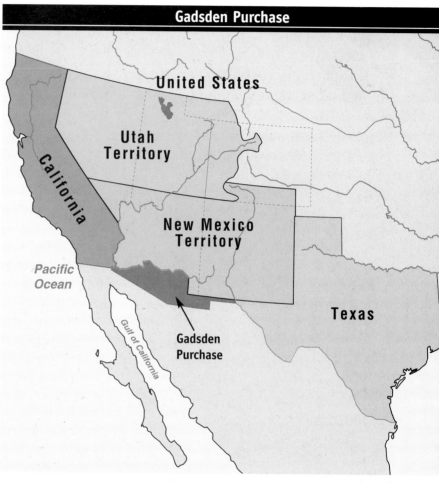

Gadsden Purchase

Today's cities of Tucson, Bisbee, Ajo, Nogales, and Yuma are on land that was part of the Gadsden Purchase.

Lesson 3

Memory Master

1. Why did U.S. armies come to Arizona?
2. What land did the United States gain as a result of the Treaty of Guadalupe Hidalgo?
3. How did the Gadsden Purchase change the shape of Arizona?

Arizona As Part of Mexico

What's the Point?

A lot of change happened in the land that was to become Arizona. When Mexico won independence from Spain, Arizona became part of Mexico.

Mountain men were the first Americans to come to Arizona. They came to trap beavers. They took the beaver pelts to trading posts. Tall felt hats made from beaver fur were popular in the East and in Europe.

Mexico was upset when Texas became part of the United States. Mexico did not want to lose Texas. The Mexican War between the United States and Mexico started. As a result of the Mexican War, the United States gained a huge piece of land in the West that had belonged to Mexico.

A few years later, the United States bought more land from Mexico. This was called the Gadsden Purchase.

Geography Tie-In

The Gadsden Purchase

On the map, find the land in Arizona that became part of the United States as a result of the Gadsden Purchase. Compare this map to a modern map. Then answer these questions:

1. Name three cities that are located on land gained from the Gadsden Purchase.

2. Was the town or city where you live part of the Gadsden Purchase?

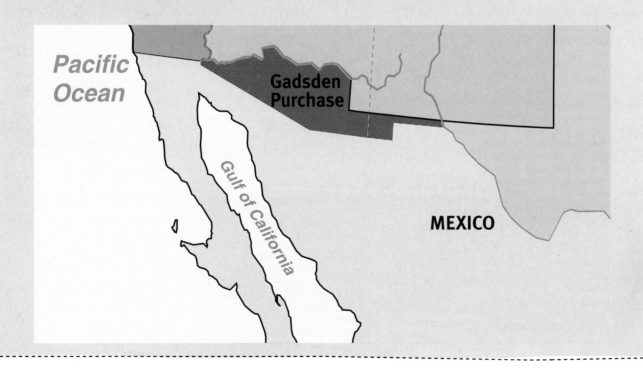

Discovering Arizona

Activity

A Chain of Events

In history, one event leads to another. In this chapter:

- Men in Europe wore tall felt hats made of beaver fur.
- Mountain men came to Arizona.
- Mountain men set traps to catch beavers.
- Mountain men took their beaver pelts to trading posts.
- Mountain men sold their pelts and bought supplies.
- People made beaver fur into tall felt hats.

On a piece of paper, draw a large circle. Then draw six smaller circles around the edge of the large circle. In each smaller circle, draw a simple picture of each of the events on the list. Draw an arrow from one circle to the next. This chain of events happened over and over again.

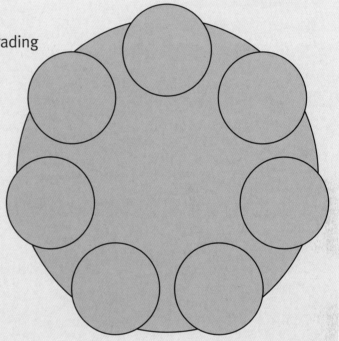

Activity

Tucson in 1860

1. Which group of people was the largest in number?
2. Which group of people was the smallest in number?
3. Why do you think there were more Mexican people than white people in Tucson?
4. Why do you think there were so few white women living in Tucson at this time?

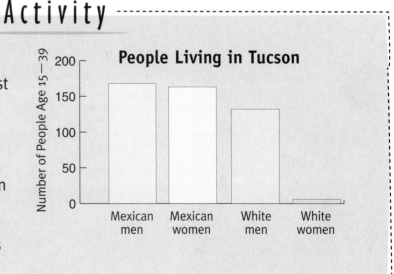

Arizona As Part of Mexico

"*The usual routine at Tubac, in addition to the regular business of getting supplies to the mining camps, was chocolate or strong coffee in the morning, breakfast at sunrise, dinner at noon, and supper at sunset.*"

—Charles Poston

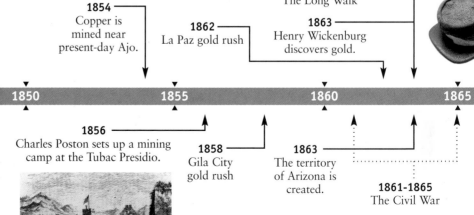

Timeline of Events

1854
Copper is mined near present-day Ajo.

1862
La Paz gold rush

1863
The Long Walk

1863
Henry Wickenburg discovers gold.

1850   1855   1860   1865

1856
Charles Poston sets up a mining camp at the Tubac Presidio.

1858
Gila City gold rush

1863
The territory of Arizona is created.

1861-1865
The Civil War

Life in Territorial Days

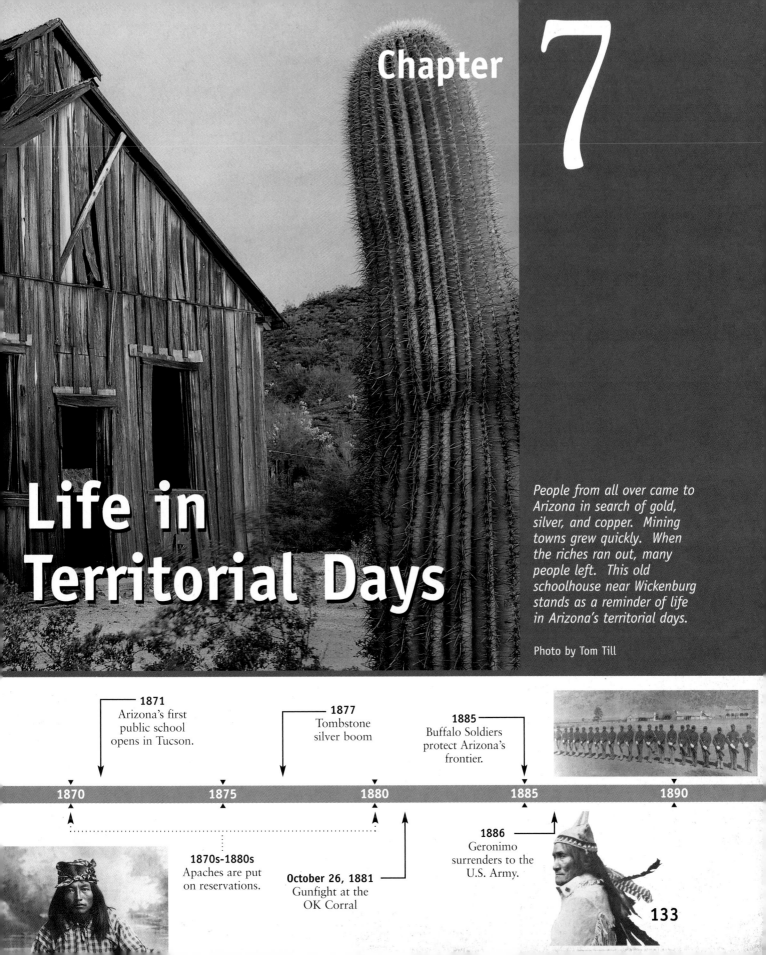

People from all over came to Arizona in search of gold, silver, and copper. Mining towns grew quickly. When the riches ran out, many people left. This old schoolhouse near Wickenburg stands as a reminder of life in Arizona's territorial days.

Photo by Tom Till

1871
Arizona's first public school opens in Tucson.

1877
Tombstone silver boom

1885
Buffalo Soldiers protect Arizona's frontier.

| 1870 | 1875 | 1880 | 1885 | 1890 |

1870s-1880s
Apaches are put on reservations.

October 26, 1881
Gunfight at the OK Corral

1886
Geronimo surrenders to the U.S. Army.

133

Early Mining Days

PEOPLE TO KNOW
Michael Goldwater
Pauline Weaver
Henry Wickenburg

PLACES TO LOCATE
Ajo
Bisbee
Clifton
Gila City
Jerome
La Paz
Morenci
Prescott
Tubac
San Francisco, California
Yuma
Wickenburg

WORDS TO KNOW
hydraulic
trough

THE NEW MEXICO TERRITORY

After the Treaty of Guadalupe Hidalgo and the Gadsden Purchase, Arizona was part of the United States. But Arizona was still not a state; it was part of the New Mexico Territory.

More people began to move here. Some came for adventure. Some came to mine gold, silver, and copper.

THE TUBAC SILVER BOOM

When the first brave Spanish explorers came to the Southwest, they were searching for glittering cities of gold. What they didn't know was that there was plenty of shiny silver, gold, and copper hidden in the ground.

In later years, a large mining boom started when silver was found near Tubac. The mines were owned by men in the East, but they hired hundreds of eager Mexican workers. Some of the silver ore was taken to Mexico on wooden wagons pulled by mules. Then it was shipped, by boat, all the way to San Francisco.

People were willing to pay a lot of money for silver. It was used to make coins, rings, necklaces, forks, knifes, and spoons.

Thousands of people moved to Tubac and other mining towns to get rich. They wanted to spend their time searching for silver, so they quickly built small log cabins or put up tents. Most people did not stay long. When the riches ran out, most people left.

The largest silver mining company set up its offices at the old Tubac Presidio.

134

GOLD RUSH TOWNS

Gila City was Arizona's first gold rush town. Gold was discovered on the Gila River near what is now Yuma. Within a year, about 1,000 people rushed in to find gold. Gila City was a village of tents and brush huts. No one wanted to spend time to build homes.

Food prices were high because people wanted to mine, not farm. Flour, beans, and vegetables had to be brought in from other places by wagon.

Pauline Weaver, one of Arizona's famous mountain men, found gold along the Colorado River near Yuma. People flocked to the spot, and a new town named La Paz was born. La Paz quickly became Arizona's largest city.

Gold was also discovered near present-day Prescott. On Rich Hill, people didn't have to dig very deep to find gold. Using a small knife, some men found gold worth thousands of dollars.

It's still possible to pan for gold in Arizona—just ask these young miners.

THE LIFE OF A MINER

Miners had a rough life. Mining was dirty work. Miners often worked in the cold and rain. There were many days when they found nothing.

Miners often owned only two shirts, two pairs of pants, strong boots, and a hat. They had to cook their own food. They carried a frying pan, a small iron pot, tin cups and plates, and a knife, fork, and spoon. They had a supply of bacon, flour, salt, baking soda, beans, and candles. If they were lucky, they had tea and sugar.

Mining Tools

A miner's simplest tool was a pan or washbowl. A miner went to a river or stream and put mud in a pan. He swished water and mud around. Gold is heavier than mud, so it sinks to the bottom.

Hydraulic mining cost a lot, but it produced a lot more gold than earlier methods.

Digging for Gold

Miners sometimes found gold underground. The miners dug a large hole with picks and shovels to get the gold.

In later years, large mining companies used water hoses. People aimed the water at mountainsides and broke down the dirt. This is called *hydraulic* mining. Then they put the dirt in a *trough* that separated the gold from the mud. This type of mining cost a lot, but it produced the most gold.

Wickenburg's Vulture Mine

"Gold!" shouted the lonely prospector to a vulture hovering above his head. Henry Wickenburg looked carefully at the metal glittering in the sun. He was standing on a gold mine. The rich ore turned out to be the largest gold deposit in the region.

The town of Wickenburg sprang to life. The J. Goldwater and other stores moved in and sold expensive supplies and food that had to be freighted in by wagon. Noisy saloons stayed open all night. Wickenburg became one of the largest towns in the territory.

The Orient Saloon was in Bisbee, a town that grew because of copper mining. Gambling was a favorite way to pass the time.

COPPER MINES

Copper soon became the most important mineral in Arizona. The electric motor, telephone, and light bulb had been invented. They all used copper wire. Electricity flows easily through copper wire.

Copper was first mined in Arizona near present-day Ajo. Hundreds of towns sprang up because of the copper boom. Jerome, Bisbee, Clifton, Morenci, and Ajo all grew quickly.

Many of the gold and silver boom towns suddenly became ghost towns when miners left to search for copper.

This man is dressed like a miner.

Memory Master

1. Describe the life of Arizona's early miners.
2. What minerals were important to the growth of Arizona? Why?
3. How was copper used in new inventions?

Life in Territorial Days

137

Lesson 2

Arizona Grows

PEOPLE TO KNOW
John Goodwin
Jacob Hamblin
Abraham Lincoln
William Murphy
Charles D. Poston
Jack Swilling

PLACES TO LOCATE
Glendale
Mesa
Picacho Pass
Prescott
Scottsdale

WORDS TO KNOW
civil
plantation

ARIZONA BECOMES A TERRITORY

The U.S. government was impressed by mining in Arizona. It finally made Arizona a separate territory from New Mexico. Leaders from Washington, D.C. chose people to be in charge of the territory.

A Governor for the Territory

President Abraham Lincoln chose John Goodwin to be the governor of the Arizona Territory. Goodwin had to choose where the capitol would be. Tucson seemed like a good place because many people already lived there, but Goodwin chose to start a new town. He picked a spot near the mines in the Bradshaw Mountains and named it Prescott. Settlers came to live in Prescott, and the town grew.

An eleven-room Governor's Mansion and a two-room capitol building were built in Prescott. The seats and tables in the capitol were made of rough boards. It had dirt floors and no windows. This was the beginning of Arizona's territorial government.

Later, Arizona's capitol moved from Prescott to Tucson, then back to Prescott. It then moved to Phoenix. This move stuck! Phoenix is still the capitol of Arizona.

The first Governor's Mansion was built in Prescott.

Discovering Arizona

The Civil War

At the same time that the mining boom was happening in the new Arizona Territory, a terrible *civil* war started in the United States. A civil war is fought between people who live in the same country.

The Civil War started because the states in the North and the South disagreed about many things. The South wanted states to have more power in the government. They also wanted to be able to keep using slaves on their huge cotton, tobacco, rice, and sugar *plantations*. Plantations are large farms. Many people in the North thought slavery was wrong.

During the war, the North was called the United States of America, or the Union. The South was called the Confederate States of America, or the Confederacy.

The southern part of Arizona became part of the Confederacy. Many people in Arizona were happy to be part of the Confederacy. They wanted Confederate soldiers to protect them from Indian attacks and outlaws. Some Arizonans did not want to be part of the Confederacy. They wanted to stay with the Union.

Most of the battles in the Civil War were fought outside of Arizona. There were many terrible battles in the East, and thousands of people were killed. There were only a few small battles in Arizona. One happened at a place called Picacho Pass, near Tucson.

This boy was ten years old when he went to fight in the Civil War. He was the youngest soldier in the Union Army.

These are some of the weapons used by Confederate soldiers. This hat was worn by a Confederate Soldier.

THE MAGIC OF WATER

Water can turn Arizona's dry desert valleys into good farmland. As you have learned, the Hohokam Indians were the first people to irrigate crops in Arizona. They dug canals in the Salt River and Gila Valleys to bring water to their fields.

In later times, settlers came to farm the land and start towns. They, too, dug canals to bring water to their farms.

Swilling's Ditch

A man named Jack Swilling lived in the mining town of Wickenburg. Miners paid high prices for food because all food had to be hauled to Arizona by wagon. There was little farming in Arizona.

Swilling wanted to solve these problems. He started a canal company to bring water to farms in the Salt River Valley. With the help of men from Wickenburg, he dug a canal. The canal was called Swilling's Ditch. Farmers began irrigating crops with water from the canals. Soon other canal companies were digging ditches on both sides of the Salt River. Since the desert got little rain, irrigation was the only way a farmer could grow crops.

A village of adobe houses grew up near Swilling's Ditch. The people grew many crops, including pumpkins. The farmers called the town Pumpkinville.

Jack Swilling

Phoenix Grows

Later, people moved to a place on higher ground than the first site of Pumpkinville. Mexican men worked in the sun, hacking away desert plants to make streets for horses, carts, and wagons. People from the farms and mines liked to "go to town" to do business and see the sites.

The village was named Phoenix after the Phoenix bird. A legend says the bird lived for 500 years. The bird then burned itself in a fire and was born again from its own ashes. Phoenix, the town, had risen from the place of the prehistoric Hohokam Indian villages.

Phoenix grew into a modern city. Within twenty years, good dirt roads ran in every direction. A railroad made trade and travel easier. It was lighted by both gas and electric streetlights. There were elementary schools, hotels, banks, and ice plants. In those days, ice was very important!

Can you imagine Phoenix as a pumpkin patch? Today it is the largest city in Arizona.

Scottsdale and Glendale Get Water

Outside of Phoenix, a large part of the Salt River Valley was still covered only with cactus. There was no water for farms. Then William Murphy and his crew built a new canal. It was hard work. Men had to shovel the dirt into wagons. Horses had to pull the wagons of heavy dirt. Finally it was ready. The canal brought water to the farming towns of Scottsdale, Glendale, and other areas.

Murphy helped the valley grow in other ways, too. He bought land in Phoenix and planted hundreds of citrus orchards. He planned places for people to live and planted trees to shade the streets. "I would like to come back a hundred years from now and see this country," he said.

Mormon families came to Arizona to farm.

MORMON TOWNS

Mormon families came from Utah to start farming towns in Arizona. They brought tools, seeds, and animals with them. Their first settlement was in Pipe Springs, north of the Grand Canyon. The land was dry. They built a fort for protection from Indians. They raised cattle and made butter and cheese.

Jacob Hamblin was a Mormon missionary to the Indians. He blazed a wagon road from Utah to the Little Colorado River. About 200 families followed the road and came to live along the river. They built earth dams and used the water to irrigate, but in the flood season, the raging river swept the dams away. This happened year after year. Finally, the people left. Today, only Joseph City remains.

Many more Mormons came from Utah. Oxen pulled their wagons to eastern Arizona and founded many towns that remain today. Woodruff, Pine, Heber, Shumway, Taylor, Snowflake, Springerville, Eager, St. Johns, Pima, and Thatcher were started by Mormons. Men built canals. They planted crops and built a school, a church, and homes.

Mormons also started the town of Lehi on the Salt River. Until the first crops were ready to eat, the families lived on fish from the river.

Mesa Grows

Mormon men began digging the Mesa Canal with the help of the Tohono O'odham Indians. They had no time to rest even though the hot summer sun, dust storms, and rattlesnakes made life miserable. They finished the canal, planted beans, wheat, corn, and vegetables, and built a town they called Mesa.

Mormons used oxen to pull their wagons full of supplies.

Farming in the heat was hard work. "I often [covered my clothes with water] before starting to hoe a row of corn . . . and before reaching the end of a row my clothes were dry," said a Mesa farmer.

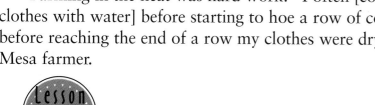

Memory Master

1. How did Phoenix get its start?
2. What did William Murphy do to help Phoenix, Scottsdale, and Glendale?
3. How did the town of Mesa get started?

Life in Territorial Days

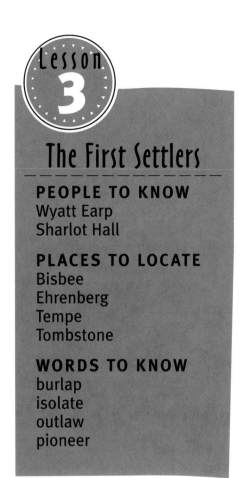

Lesson

3

The First Settlers

PEOPLE TO KNOW
Wyatt Earp
Sharlot Hall

PLACES TO LOCATE
Bisbee
Ehrenberg
Tempe
Tombstone

WORDS TO KNOW
burlap
isolate
outlaw
pioneer

LIFE IN PIONEER TOWNS

Many *pioneers* came to live and work in Arizona. A pioneer is one of the first people to do something. The Mormons that came to Arizona were some of the pioneers that helped Arizona grow. Pioneers were *isolated* from other people. Farm and ranch houses were miles apart. Families lived far away from any large cities.

Clothes

The Mexican people adapted to the hot climate better than other pioneers did. Mexican women wore loose short-sleeved cotton dresses. Many of the Mexican men wore sandals and light cotton clothes to beat the heat. They wore the wide-brimmed *sombrero* hat to shade their faces.

Other pioneer women suffered in their long-sleeved dresses with high collars. The men wore long-sleeved shirts, wool pants and socks, and leather boots. All adults wore hats. Children dressed in smaller versions of adult clothes. Girls never wore pants. No one wore shorts.

Even though it was hot outside, many pioneer women wore long, heavy dresses. This Tucson family is dressed in their Sunday best.

Lighting

In the early days, pioneers used candles for light in their homes. Some people used a burning rag dipped in a saucer of grease. Coal oil lamps were used, but they were smoky and dangerous.

Later, gas lights glowed in stores and on streets. Even later, there were some electric lights in Phoenix and Tucson, but homes did not get electricity until much later.

Beating the Heat

Summers were hot in the desert towns. Homes had thick adobe walls to keep the heat out. Adobe was made of clay that had been dried in the sun. When wood was available, people built a wide porch to shade the walls. They sprinkled water on dirt floors during hot summer days to keep them from getting dusty.

The Hotel Adams in Phoenix had an unusual cooling system. Huge blocks of ice were placed in pans around the lobby. Large fans blew air over the ice to spread out the cool air.

Most families had a homemade desert refrigerator outside. A wooden frame was covered with **burlap** on all sides. The burlap was kept damp by water dripping from a bucket on top. The wind served as the fan. It was surprising how well this desert refrigerator kept milk, butter, and meat from spoiling.

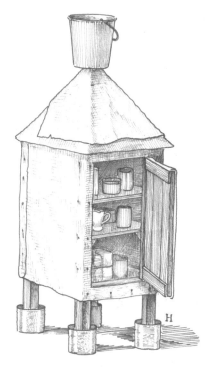
A desert refrigerator kept food cool.

Money

The pioneers used money that was different from what we use today. The first bank bills were called "horse blankets" because they were so large. They were almost twice as large as one of today's dollar bills.

Some Arizona bankers carried uncut sheets of paper money. When they made a purchase, they asked the clerk for scissors. They cut off the number of bills needed.

Coins were in short supply. Many saloons and other businesses used tokens instead of coins. The tokens helped to advertise a place of business. The printing on a token told what it could buy or how much it was worth in trade at a store or saloon.

Can you tell what this token would buy?

Special Days

There were times for fun in the frontier towns. The Fourth of July was a special day. Most towns had parades. Families had picnics. One year, the parade in Tucson was one mile long.

Fire-hose team races were popular in some towns. Each team pulled a two-wheeled fire hose cart to a hydrant. The hose was hooked up and the water turned on. The team with the fastest time won. The races helped the people practice for times when they would need to put out fires.

In mining towns, the hard-rock drilling contest was a popular event. One man held a steel drill. His partner drove it into a block of stone with a sledge hammer. The holder risked getting his hand smashed, but the prizes were big. One year the winners in Bisbee got $800. They drilled a record hole of nearly forty-seven inches.

One favorite Mexican holiday was Cinco de Mayo. It celebrates the Mexican victory over French troops. In the battle, a small group of Mexican men defeated the more well-equipped French troops. The Mexicans won, and their victory gave hope to all Mexicans. It proved that Mexico had the strength to fight a great power. To celebrate the holiday, some Arizona towns had parades. People still celebrate Cinco de Mayo today!

In Flagstaff, fire-hose team races helped men prepare for times when they would have to put out real fires.

Discovering Arizona

Early Schools

The first school in Arizona was the San Xavier mission school near Tucson. Two Mexican Catholic priests started the school. In Tucson, Mexican boys learned English at one school. Girls could go to a private Catholic school if their families could pay the fees. However, most children didn't go to school at all.

Early schools had only one room where all the grades met together. They didn't have many books, and they didn't have much paper. The students often wrote on slates. A slate is a small blackboard. Students drank water from a dipper in a bucket. Bathrooms were outdoor "privies."

Another schoolhouse in Tucson was a one-room adobe building. The dirt floor had to be sprinkled with water to keep down the dust. The benches were rough and splintery.

In Ehrenberg and Tempe, schools were opened in old saloons. The teacher in Ehrenberg wrote that old miners would wander into her school. They did not know it was no longer a saloon.

The first school in Bisbee was an old miner's shack. It had a dirt floor but no doors or windows. Desks were made by laying boards on boxes. The seats were planks placed on old nail barrels.

> "Our little country schoolhouse was one large room. A wood shed was attached to the rear. We . . . used to walk the two miles to and from school each day, oftentimes through snow and cold."
>
> —*Evelyn Mackin Zuchero,*

Students and parents gathered at Scottsdale's first school.

Ed Schieffelin found silver in a place he called Tombstone. People said he would never find silver, only his tombstone. Within two years, Tombstone had one of the largest mining rushes in American history. The town grew quickly.

ARIZONA PORTRAIT

Sharlot Hall
1870–1943

Sharlot Hall heard many stories from the first settlers. She thought that the history of Arizona was important. She began saving items that belonged to pioneers and Native Americans.

She became Arizona's first territorial historian. This made her the first woman to hold a paid office in the territory.

Sharlot liked to write poetry and short stories. She sold her first story for four dollars. Later, she published over 500 stories and poems.

Sharlot's collection can still be seen today. The Sharlot Hall Museum in Prescott shows what life was like in Arizona Territory. Some of the photographs in this book are from her museum.

OUTLAWS

In the early days, most Arizona towns had to deal with *outlaws.* Tombstone is famous for its gunmen, robbers, cattle stealers, and gamblers. Tombstone, however, was not really much worse than other towns. Most of the people in Tombstone obeyed the law. The town had churches and schools.

Wyatt Earp was the leader of the Earp family in Tombstone. He did not like the sheriff and the Clanton family. They argued a lot. The Earps had a famous shoot-out with the Clanton gang. This street fight was near the OK Corral. It became known as the "wild west's best-remembered gunfight."

Wyatt Earp was part of the famous shoot-out at the OK Corral.

Lesson 3

Memory Master

1. List some ways people "beat the heat."

2. Compare pioneer clothes to what you wear today.

3. How were early schools different than schools today?

THE CATTLE INDUSTRY

There was little ranching in Arizona before the Civil War. Most of the cattle were just passing through. People drove large herds of Texas longhorn cattle across Arizona to California.

The Ranching Boom

After the Civil War, hundreds of cattle ranchers came to Arizona. Henry Hooker was one of the most successful. He drove in large herds of Texas longhorns so he could sell beef to the U.S. Army and to Indians on the reservations.

Hooker found a good place for a ranch in the Sulphur Springs Valley. He called it the Sierra Bonita Ranch. In a few years, Hooker controlled hundreds of miles of land.

There were many other big ranches in southern Arizona. One of the most famous was the Empire Ranch. Their *brand* was a heart.

Longhorn cattle from Texas passed through Arizona.

Lesson 4

Ranching in Arizona

PEOPLE TO KNOW
Henry Hooker

PLACES TO LOCATE
Flagstaff
Holbrook
Yuma

WORDS TO KNOW
brand
commercial

"We got to town about once a year. Sometimes we wouldn't be paid for a year. Our diet was mixed. In the summer we had beef and beans. In the winter we had jerky and beans."

—*Harry Heffner, a cattleman from the Empire Ranch*

Cattle were rounded up at Sierra Bonita Ranch.

Life in Territorial Days

149

Can you see the branding iron in this picture?

Branding

Ranchers let their cattle graze on public lands. Since so many ranchers used the same grazing land, ranchers branded their cattle so they would know whom each cow belonged to. They burned a symbol into the cow's hide with a hot branding iron.

Examples of brands include a box, circle, diamond, bar, triangle, heart, cross, rocking chair, umbrella, half-moon, coffeepot, violin, and many Mexican designs.

Too Many Cows

Before herds of cattle came, Arizona's valleys were covered with grasses. Some grass grew as high as a horse's belly. The grass allowed rain to soak slowly into the ground.

Soon, too many cattle were roaming on the grasslands.

Discovering Arizona

They were destroying the grasslands by eating too much grass. Soil that was once held in place by grass roots began to wash away.

Ranching methods slowly started to change. Ranchers did not let as many cows graze on the open range.

Cattle Ranching in Northern Arizona

The cattle industry also grew in northern Arizona. The A-One was the largest ranch near Flagstaff. It belonged to the Arizona Cattle Company.

Holbrook was another center of ranching. The largest ranch was the Hashknife Ranch. The Hashknife Ranch stretched along the railroad from Holbrook almost to Flagstaff. At one time, it had 60,000 cattle.

The Cowboy: Fact and Fiction

Have you ever seen an old Western movie or read a Western book? The American idea of cowboys is different from what their lives were really like. Magazines and movies show that their lives were full of adventure.

Actually, cowboys' lives were lonely. They worked long hours. They built and repaired fences, cleaned corrals, cared for sick cattle, branded cattle, milked cows, took care of horses, and carried heavy supplies. Cowboys moved from ranch to ranch. They had little education and were not paid much for all their work. Most cowboys liked their life. They loved living outdoors.

THE SHEEP INDUSTRY

Sheep ranching was important in Northern Arizona. The Hopi and Navajo had learned sheep raising from the Spanish. But the *commercial* sheep industry started when people from New Mexico brought their sheep to this part of Arizona. They raised sheep for their wool.

Later, people from California brought their sheep to Arizona. Flagstaff became the center of the sheep industry. The Daggs brothers had the largest ranch. They took care of about fifty thousand sheep. The Babbitt brothers also had a lot of sheep. It was said that the sound coming from all of their sheep was "Baa-ab-itt. Baa-ab-itt."

By the late 1870s, a lot of wool was shipped from Arizona to many places across the country. "A barge with 26 bales of wool arrived in Yuma from upriver. The Lord & Williams wagon train arrived with 39 bales."

—*Arizona Sentinel (Yuma)*

Discovering Arizona

THE OSTRICH INDUSTRY

"One egg or two?" This was a favorite joke on ostrich ranches because one ostrich egg weighs three pounds and can easily feed a dozen people.

Ostrich farms did well near Phoenix and Yuma. Each bird produced two pounds of feathers a year. Feathers were sold for between $20 and $30 a pound.

Ostrich feathers were used in women's hats, scarves, and feather dusters. The ostrich industry did well until the feathers went out of style.

People still have ostrich farms in Arizona. Some towns have ostrich festivals. Would you like to ride an ostrich?

Ostriches could be sold for more money than cattle. They also ate less, so it was cheaper for people to raise them.

Photo by James P. Rowan

Lesson 4

Memory Master

1. Why did ranchers brand their cows?
2. What happened when too many cows roamed the grasslands?
3. What city became the center of the sheep industry?
4. How did people use ostrich feathers?

Lesson 5

Indian-White Conflict

PEOPLE TO KNOW
Buffalo Soldiers
Kit Carson
George Crook
Chiricahua Apaches
Cochise
Mangas Coloradas
George Crook
Geronimo

PLACES TO LOCATE
Oklahoma
Fort Buchanan
Canyon de Chelly

WORDS TO KNOW
invasion
surrender

"We were passing the usual quiet Sunday in Tubac when a Mexican vaquero came galloping in the plaza crying out "Apaches! Apaches! Apaches! The Apaches had attacked [a big ranch] and killed the settlers."

—*Charles D. Poston*

PEACE OR WAR?

As you have read, different groups of Native Americans, explorers, mountain men, soldiers, and pioneers often got along peacefully. Indians helped the Spanish priests and explorers find food. Indians worked to build the missions. Indian guides led explorers through Arizona. The Pima helped the Mormon pioneers build a canal.

In turn, the Spanish priests taught Indians to raise cattle. They opened schools for Indian children. Spanish leaders gave food to Indian families. Mountain men often married Indian women and lived in Indian camps. Pioneers and Indians traded with each other for furs, food, guns, clothes, and jewelry.

Bad Times

Things were not always peaceful, however. Different tribes of Native Americans sometimes fought with each other. Indians often stole cattle and horses. White people took over the land that Indians had been living on for hundreds of years. Sometimes white people broke their promises to the Indians. New diseases such as smallpox and measles killed thousands of Indians. People on both sides were killed with guns or arrows.

The most important fact, however, was that after the Spanish and pioneers came to Arizona, life for the Indians was never the same again.

APACHE RAIDS

The Apache lived in what is now eastern Arizona and western New Mexico. For hundreds of years, they had lived by hunting, gathering, some farming, and raiding. They did not like the *invasion* of outsiders. They wanted to keep their way of life.

THE U.S. ARMY

The army was important in Arizona. Soldiers protected settlements and wagon trains. They usually tried to make peace by giving Indians food and clothing. They also tried to force the

Indians onto reservations. The work was dangerous. Soldiers were killed in battles. They suffered from the heat and were homesick. Often they had nothing to do in the forts.

Fort Buchanan

The army built forts to protect the settlers from Indian attacks. Fort Buchanan was built in a valley near Tubac. However, mosquitoes were bad during the rainy season. The buildings were hot, and the mud roofs leaked during wet weather.

The soldiers went into Apache country. They destroyed Indian crops and killed a few men. Then their captain offered the Apache corn and beef for signing a peace treaty. But Apaches still drove away horses and cattle from ranches, mines, and even the forts.

After the Civil War started, the soldiers left to fight the war in the East, and the forts were closed. Bands of Apaches forced nearly every rancher and miner to pack quickly and leave. Some hurried to Tucson for safety.

Soldiers Return

After a while, both Union and Confederate soldiers came to Arizona. As Union soldiers rode through Apache Pass, Indians fired on them from behind rocks.

The Apache leaders were Mangas Coloradas (Red Sleeves) and Cochise. The Apache were finally driven out by gunfire. Sixty-six Indians were killed and others wounded. Two soldiers died. "You never would have whipped us if you had not used the wagons that shoot," Cochise said. He was talking about cannons.

After that, soldiers built a fort at Apache Pass to protect wagon trains, stagecoaches, and cattle herders.

"At the break of day, the Apaches gave a whoop and [took] the entire herd—146 horses and mules—before the astonished gaze of five watchmen, who were sleeping under a porch."
—*Charles D. Poston*

Mangas Coloradas became chief of the Apache when he was almost fifty years old.

Life in Territorial Days

155

Apache Reservations

White and Mexican settlers were tired of being afraid of the Apache. Many had had family members killed. They wanted soldiers to force all of the Apache onto reservations. A peaceful Indian agent was sent to make treaties with the Indians. Finally, all the major Apache bands but one lived on reservations.

The Chiricahuas were the only Apache group who did not live on a reservation. Cochise, one of their leaders, had fought the settlers for years. He finally agreed to a treaty. The Indians were promised food, clothing, and land. The Chiricahuas walked hundreds of miles to the reservation in New Mexico. "The white man and the Indian are to drink the same water and eat the same bread," said Cochise.

The Chiricahuas were unhappy on the reservation. They didn't have enough food. They didn't like living with different Indian bands who had been enemies before. Many of the Apache escaped with Geronimo and went to Mexico. They were finally caught and sent back to the reservation.

Small Apache groups escaped again and again. Finally, after Geronimo surrendered, he and all of the Chiricahuas were sent by train all the way to Florida. This way, the soldiers thought, they could not escape. They were later moved to Oklahoma, but they never came back to Arizona.

Some Apaches, like Geronimo, did not want to surrender to the U.S. Army and live on a reservation.

Apache Scouts

Not all Chiricahua Apaches fought against Army soldiers. Some of them became scouts for the U.S. Army. The Apache scouts were hired to track Apache warriors who killed settlers. The scouts were paid money from the Army.

General George Crook was in charge of the Apache scouts. He wanted to have peace with the people. He said, "If your people will only behave yourselves and stop killing the whites, I will be the best friend you ever had. I will teach you to work, and will find you a market for everything you can sell."

"Dutchy" was a Chiricahua Apache scout for the U.S. Army.

Discovering Arizona

BUFFALO SOLDIERS

After the Civil War, African American soldiers joined the U.S. Army and were sent to the West. The Indians called them Buffalo Soldiers because their short curly hair looked like a buffalo coat. The buffalo was an important animal to the Indians. The name Buffalo Soldiers was a sign of respect.

The Buffalo Soldiers worked to protect pioneers and towns. They captured outlaws and fought Indians and cattle thieves. In their time protecting the West, thirteen Buffalo Soldiers earned Medals of Honor from the government.

Two soldiers earned the Medal of Honor for guarding the army payroll. Robbers had blocked the road with a huge rock. When the soldiers stopped to move the rock, the robbers fired down from a rocky ledge. They forced the soldiers to retreat to a dry creek bed and leave the gold and silver in the wagon. In the fight, eight soldiers were hit. The Buffalo Soldiers returned fire even after they were badly hurt. The robbers ended up stealing the payroll, but the Buffalo Soldiers were honored for their courage during the fight.

Buffalo Soldiers searched for Geronimo. They also fought small battles with the Apache. The soldiers were given the sad job of gathering 400 peaceful Apaches and putting them on a train for Florida.

Buffalo soldiers protected the Arizona frontier.

Life in Territorial Days

Geronimo

Geronimo was an important Apache warrior. When he was very old, Geronimo told the story of his life to someone who wrote it down. Here are some of the things he said:

I was born in Arizona . . . among the mountains. When a child, my mother taught me of the sun and sky, the moon and stars, the clouds and storms. She also taught me to kneel and pray to Usen [God] for strength, wisdom, and protection.

With my brothers and sisters I played hide-and-seek among the rocks and pines. Sometimes we rested in the shade of the cottonwood trees. Sometimes we played that we were warriors. My father had often told me of the brave deeds of our warriors.

When we were old enough . . . we went to the field with our parents. We broke the ground with wooden hoes. We planted the corn in straight rows, the beans among the corn, and the melons and pumpkins. In the autumn, the harvest was carried on the backs of ponies up to our homes.

A Warrior's Life

When Geronimo was seventeen years old, he was admitted to the council of warriors. This meant he was a man and could go to battle. He was also able to marry.

Perhaps the greatest joy to me was that now I could marry the fair Alope. . . . I appeared before her father's wigwam with the herd of ponies and took with me Alope. . . . I had made for us a new home. The tepee was made of buffalo hides and in it were many bear robes . . . and spears, bows, and arrows. Alope drew many pictures on the walls. . . . Three children came to us.

For many years, Geronimo made friends with U.S. soldiers. At other times, he raided white and Mexican settlements. He and his band sometimes killed people or took them captive. One day, while he was away from his home, Mexican soldiers killed Geronimo's family. Geronimo was deeply saddened and vowed revenge. He took part in more raids against settlers and soldiers. Later he said, "I could not call back my loved ones, but I could take revenge."

For years, the raids went on. The U.S. soldiers tried to put the Apache on reservations. Geronimo was sent to the reservation in New Mexico, but he escaped. He left with a group of men, women, and children. They headed for Mexico, raiding along the way.

Hundreds of soldiers went to find Geronimo. Finally, he *surrendered*. He was sent to Florida for a few years, then to a reservation in Oklahoma.

Geronimo's Later Life

While in Oklahoma, Geronimo was taken to the world's fair in St. Louis. He joined the Wild West Show. People came from all over the country to see him. He wore special clothes, feathers, and jewelry. He sold pictures of himself and autographs for a quarter. He sold buttons off his shirt. Later, Geronimo even rode in a parade for the president of the United States.

I am glad I went to the fair. I learned . . . the white people . . . are very kind and peaceful people. I wish all my people could have attended the fair.

After the long walk, soldiers watched over the Navajo.

The Navajo hid from U.S. soldiers in Canyon de Chelly. Soldiers chased them through the canyon and forced them onto a reservation in New Mexico.

THE LONG WALK

Towards the end of the Civil War, the leader of the Union Army began rounding up the Navajo and some Apache bands. He forced them to live on the same reservation in New Mexico.

Kit Carson and his soldiers were ordered to find all the Navajo and force them to leave their homes. They burned many of the Indian's crops and killed their livestock. More than 8,000 men, women, and children walked hundreds of miles in the winter. They did not have enough food or warm clothes. Many died. The journey was called the "Long Walk."

Life in New Mexico was hard. The people missed their homes in Arizona. They did not like living with the Apache.

After several years, they were allowed to return to their homelands. They left the reservation in New Mexico and made the long journey to their new reservation in Arizona.

Lesson 5

Memory Master

1. Why was the U.S. Army important in Arizona?

2. What were some of the reasons the Indians did not want to live on reservations?

3. Describe some of what you read about Geronimo.

Discovering Arizona

What's the Point?

Arizona was part of the New Mexico Territory. Later, that territory was divided and the place you live now was part of the Arizona Territory.

Silver, gold, and copper were discovered. People came to work in the mines and get rich. Other people came to raise cattle. Pioneers came for a different reason. They came to farm and start towns. They built canals to bring water from the rivers to farms. Phoenix and other towns grew.

Life in the territory was not always peaceful. Native Americans did not like the new people moving to their tribal lands. They often stole cattle. People on both sides were killed. Soldiers came to keep the peace. Finally, the Native Americans were moved to reservations. It was a sad time for the Indian people.

Activity

Being a Pioneer

You have just read about pioneer life in the Arizona Territory. Pretend that you are a pioneer. Write a journal entry about your life. Use some of the following questions to get you started:

- What do you like about your life as a pioneer?
- What is your school like?
- What work do your parents do?
- What chores do you have to do?
- What do you wish was different?

Activity

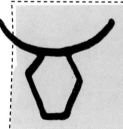

Make Your Own Brand

Ranchers often designed their own brands. The designs were simple. Look at these examples.

Pretend that you are an early rancher. Design your own brand. Explain where you got the idea for your design.

Geography Tie-In

People and the Land

In this chapter, you learned that cattlemen let too many cows graze on the grasslands. The cows started to ruin the land. Cattlemen solved this problem by not letting as many cows graze on the land.

What are some things people do today that harm the land? Can you think of ways that people could protect the land?

Life in Territorial Days

"*The horseless carriage will never, of course, come into as common use as the bicycle.*"

—*Literary Digest, 1900*

Timeline of Events

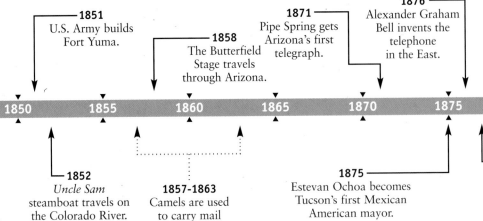

1851
U.S. Army builds
Fort Yuma.

1858
The Butterfield
Stage travels
through Arizona.

1871
Pipe Spring gets
Arizona's first
telegraph.

1876
Alexander Graham
Bell invents the
telephone
in the East.

1850   1855   1860   1865   1870   1875

1852
Uncle Sam
steamboat travels on
the Colorado River.

1857-1863
Camels are used
to carry mail
and supplies.

1875
Estevan Ochoa becomes
Tucson's first Mexican
American mayor.

Arizona Reaches Out

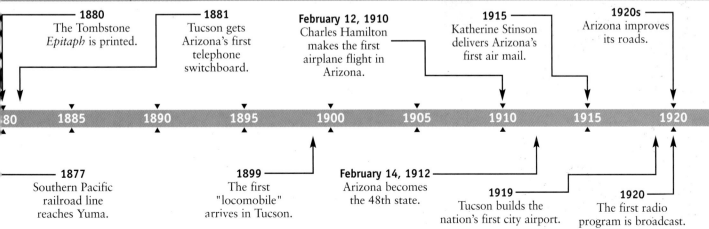

Three families take a ride near Prescott in the early 1900s. There were few roads then.

1880
The Tombstone *Epitaph* is printed.

1881
Tucson gets Arizona's first telephone switchboard.

February 12, 1910
Charles Hamilton makes the first airplane flight in Arizona.

1915
Katherine Stinson delivers Arizona's first air mail.

1920s
Arizona improves its roads.

| 80 | 1885 | 1890 | 1895 | 1900 | 1905 | 1910 | 1915 | 1920 |

1877
Southern Pacific railroad line reaches Yuma.

1899
The first "locomobile" arrives in Tucson.

February 14, 1912
Arizona becomes the 48th state.

1919
Tucson builds the nation's first city airport.

1920
The first radio program is broadcast.

Arizona Becomes a State

PEOPLE TO KNOW
George W. P. Hunt
Abraham Lincoln
William Howard Taft

PLACES TO LOCATE
Bisbee
Globe
Yuma
Washington, D.C.

WORDS TO KNOW
communication
telegram
transportation

A telegram was a message received by pulses on an electric wire. Telegrams helped Arizona communicate with the rest of the country.

AN IMPORTANT MESSAGE

When President Abraham Lincoln made Arizona a territory, there were not many people living here. There was no easy way for people to travel to Arizona.

It was hard for people to get news and supplies from other parts of the country or other parts of the territory. You couldn't easily send a letter between Tucson and Yuma.

In time, the Arizona Territory grew. On February 14, 1912, an important *telegram* arrived all the way from Washington, D.C. President William Howard Taft had made Arizona a state.

The news traveled fast. Steam whistles were heard everywhere. In Globe, a cannon sounded forty-eight times. People from Bisbee exploded dynamite on Copper Queen Mountain. There were parades in Phoenix and other towns.

What had helped Arizona grow so much? Why was it easier for people to come to the west? Things had changed. Arizona had a good railroad system. About 1,800 Arizonans owned automobiles. Airplanes were beginning to fly over the state. These improvements in *transportation* and *communication* helped Arizona grow.

President Taft signed a law to make Arizona the 48th state. The news traveled fast.

164

Discovering Arizona

Transportation and Communication

Transportation means moving people or goods from one place to another. It was important in helping Arizona grow. Communication is giving and receiving information. Today, people talk with each other on the phone. A mail carrier brings letters to homes. Radio, TV, newspapers, and the Internet bring us news from around the world. These are all forms of communication.

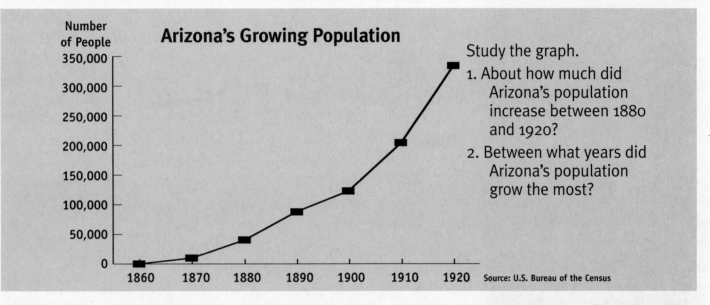

Arizona's Growing Population

Source: U.S. Bureau of the Census

Study the graph.
1. About how much did Arizona's population increase between 1880 and 1920?
2. Between what years did Arizona's population grow the most?

THE STATE'S FIRST GOVERNOR

Shortly after he heard Arizona was a state, George W. P. Hunt walked to the capitol in Phoenix. Hunt had helped run the Arizona Territory. Now he would become the state's first governor.

Hunt had arrived in Arizona as a poor young man. In time, he became a rich banker. As governor, he remembered his hard times, and he fought for better working conditions for people. He served a total of twenty years as governor of Arizona.

George W.P. Hunt was Arizona State's first governor.

Lesson 1

Memory Master

1. How did Arizona get the news about becoming a state?
2. What is transportation? What is communication?
3. Who was Arizona's first governor?

Lesson 2

Early Transportation

PEOPLE TO KNOW
Edward Beale
John Butterfield
Mormon Battalion
Estevan Ochoa

PLACES TO LOCATE
Pennsylvania
San Francisco, California
St. Louis, Missouri

WORDS TO KNOW
freight
stagecoach
toll road

"We found that the only way to get through was to travel slowly in the cool of the day. . . . The dust was generally from six to twelve inches deep."
—*Louisiana Stretzel*

ROADS

Before Arizona became a state, it needed better, faster ways for people to travel. Arizona's first wagon road was made by men in the Mormon Battalion. It became known as the Gila Trail. Many people going to California used the road. They passed through Tucson and Yuma.

Later, some **toll roads** were built in Arizona. People had to pay each time they used the road. The charge was four cents a mile for a wagon. A rider on horseback paid two-and-a-half cents a mile.

Butterfield Overland Mail Company

The Butterfield Overland Mail Company had the first good *stagecoach* line across Arizona. It ran from St. Louis, Missouri, to San Francisco, California. Part of the stagecoach line followed the old Gila Trail.

Stagecoaches carried passengers and mail. John Butterfield never wanted the mail to be late. He told his drivers, "Remember, boys, nothing on earth can stop the U.S. mail." The mail was late only three times.

The trip from St. Louis to San Francisco took twenty-five days. The trip was hard because the dirt roads were often dusty, muddy, or rocky. People bounced up and down on the hard seats.

The average speed was five miles an hour. Sometimes outlaws stopped the stages and robbed the passengers.

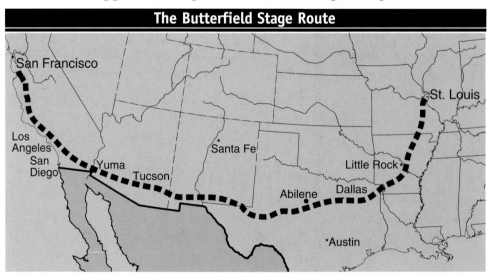

The Butterfield Stage Route

Stagecoach Stations

Most of the stagecoach stations in Arizona were built of adobe. A wall around the station gave protection from Indian attacks. Stations had fresh horses or mules and extra stagecoaches. There was hay and corn for the animals and food for the passengers.

Stage stations did not have the best food. They usually served jerky, stale bread, and beans. The story is told about one salesman who would not eat the beans at one Arizona stage stop. He demanded better food, but a local man put a Colt's revolver in his face and said, "Stranger, eat them beans!" And he did.

A stagecoach ride was full of adventure! This stagecoach ran between Flagstaff and the Grand Canyon.

Wagons brought their loads to this freight station in Tucson.
Photo by James P. Rowan

WAGON FREIGHTING

Moving *freight* from one city to another was important. Books, food, chairs, tables, soap, and clothes were all freight. Anything that people needed from other places was freight. Before the railroads came, freight was carried in wagons.

Travel was slow. A pioneer merchant said it took two to three months to get goods from San Francisco to his store in Tucson. It took as long as six months to get goods from the East to his store.

Oxen pulled freight wagons into Arizona.

THE GREAT CAMEL EXPERIMENT

The U.S. government asked Lieutenant Edward Beale to find out all he could about camels. They thought camels could carry freight and mail in the deserts of the West. Beale thought it was a great idea.

Camels could carry heavy loads and walk long distances without needing water. Beale planned a race between camels and mules. He divided a 2.5 ton load between six camels and twelve mules. Each team carried their load for 60 miles. The camels finished in just over two days, but it took the mules four days to finish.

But camels were not perfect. The strange-smelling camels scared the horses and mules. And sometimes, the camels did not know how to follow orders and went the wrong way.

Soon, the experiment ended. Most of the camels were sold, but some were let loose. For many years, newspapers wrote stories about wild camels seen in the desert.

Camels helped carry mail to Arizona.

Lesson 2 · Memory Master

1. What type of roads cost money to travel on?

2. What was it like to ride in a stagecoach?

3. Why did Edward Beale think camels could carry mail and freight in the desert?

ARIZONA PORTRAIT

Estevan Ochoa
1831–1888

Estevan Ochoa came to Arizona from Mexico. As a young boy he worked on freight trains. He learned how to speak English on the trains.

Later, he moved to Tucson and started a freighting business. His freighting company became the largest one in Arizona. It transported goods from as far away as Pennsylvania. Ochoa's company employed hundreds of men in Pima County.

Ochoa also supported education. He let schools be built on some of his land. He was a very important man in Tucson. He was the first Mexican American mayor of Tucson.

This train went to Phoenix. It stopped in Wickenburg to get water.

PEOPLE TO KNOW
Edward E. Ayers
Hiram Fenner
Charles Hamilton
Fred Harvey
Charles Lindbergh
Katherine Stinson

PLACES TO LOCATE
China
Japan
Ash Fork
Benson
Casa Grande
Flagstaff
Holbrook
Kingman
Seligman
Willcox
Williams
Winslow

WORDS TO KNOW
barnstormer
concrete
dedicate
steamboat

RAILROADS

Some of the most important events of pioneer days were the arrival of the railroads. Railroads helped carry heavy loads to and from businesses. Products from mines and ranches could be sent to market quickly and easily by train.

People could also travel on trains through Arizona, as well as the rest of the country, in comfort, safety, and speed.

The Southern Pacific Railroad

The first major railroad in Arizona was the Southern Pacific. Many Chinese and Mexican men came for jobs building the railroads. They laid tracks east of Yuma. At Casa Grande, they stopped building the railroad for a while because of the hot weather. Many workers were laid off. Some of the Chinese men went to Phoenix to live.

In 1880, a train finally arrived in Tucson. It blew its loud whistle. Workers drove a spike made from Tombstone silver into the ground. A crowd of people looked on.

The Southern Pacific Company built more tracks. Many stations along the railroad line became important towns. Some of these were Casa Grande, Benson, and Willcox.

These men are laying railroad tracks. It was hard work in Arizona's hot deserts.

Chinese Workers and the Railroad

Many Chinese men came to the United States to work for railroad companies. Some of them came to Arizona. When work on the railroads ended, Chinese men and their families stayed in Arizona.

Chinatowns grew in Prescott, Tucson, and Phoenix. Chinese people had a place to share their music, food, religion, and other customs. Many Chinese-owned grocery stores and laundry shops did well in Phoenix and Tucson.

People from Japan also came to Arizona. Japanese farmers grew vegetables and cotton outside of Phoenix and Tucson. One Japanese family was the first to raise strawberries in Arizona.

Lee Tan had a grocery store in Tucson.

Arizona Reaches Out

The Santa Fe Railroad

An important railroad ran across northern Arizona. Towns grew along the Santa Fe Railroad. Winslow, Holbrook, Flagstaff, Williams, Ash Fork, Seligman, and Kingman were some of them.

In Flagstaff, Edward E. Ayers built a huge sawmill. He made railroad ties for the Santa Fe Railroad. He also shipped his lumber to mines and towns in Arizona.

Most of the towns near the railroads had a Harvey House restaurant. Travelers could get a good meal there. The service was good, too. Fred Harvey hired young ladies from the East as waitresses. They were called "Harvey Girls."

These girls were given a free train ride to their jobs in the West. The railroad company also built the restaurants and hauled Harvey's food without charge. Why? The Harvey House was good for railroad business.

These waitresses were called "Harvey Girls."

Can you tell which picture of Flagstaff was taken before the railroad came?

The Santa Fe Railroad brought goods and people to Arizona towns.

Discovering Arizona

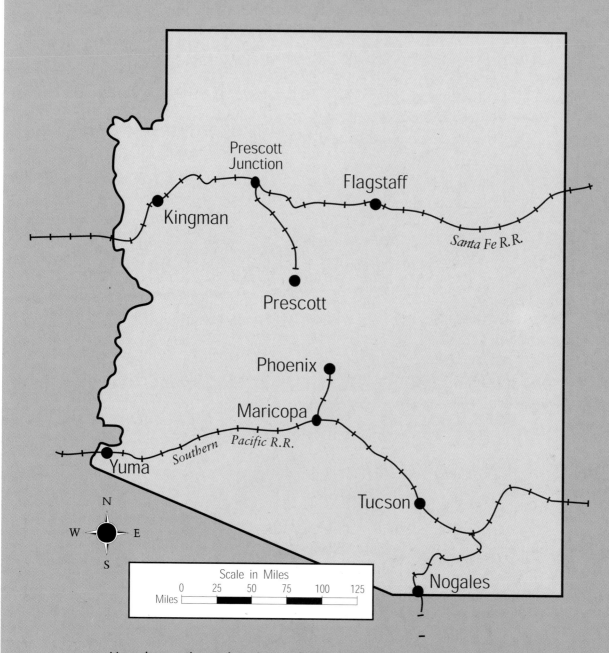

Use the scale and a piece of string to measure distance on the map. Then answer these questions:

1. About how many miles is it from Flagstaff to Prescott Junction?

2. If a train was traveling at 30 miles per hour, how long would it take to go from Yuma to Maricopa?

STEAMBOATS

Before railroads came to Arizona, *steamboats* carried supplies. The steamboats arrived in Arizona on sailing ships. The steamboats were put together at the Colorado River.

Steamboats had a large paddle wheel on the side or rear of the boat. A large engine turned the paddle wheel. This wheel moved the boat through the water. They could travel 15 miles in one day.

The *Uncle Sam* was the first steamboat to sail up the Colorado River. It hauled freight from the mouth of the Colorado to Fort Yuma. Many towns received supplies from steamboats. It was easier to carry freight on a steamboat than across the land. People rode on the boats, too.

Yuma Grows

As Arizona grew, there was more need for supplies. The U.S. Army set up Fort Yuma to protect the place where the Colorado and Gila Rivers met. The Colorado River was not as wide there as it was in other places, so it was easier to cross the river. Large ships with supplies sailed up the Gulf of California to the mouth of the Colorado River. Then steamboats took the supplies to Fort Yuma.

People began moving to Fort Yuma. They settled a town on the Arizona side of the Colorado River. Later, people named the town Yuma. Yuma became a busy city. Steamboats unloaded many supplies. Almost all of the goods that came to Arizona came through Yuma.

At Yuma, people sometimes took a steamboat ride just for fun.

174

AUTOMOBILES ARRIVE

The first automobiles were more like toys. They did not do too well on rough roads. The first gas buggies were sold by bicycle stores and wagon makers. Drugstores sold gas and oil. Soon, horse stables were changed to garages.

Driving was not always pleasant in the early days. The roads were bad, tires went flat easily, and engines had little power. Drivers had to have a few spare tires, a tow rope, grease, an oil can, and a tire repair kit. Most of the cars were open, with only a canvas top. Rain was not a welcome event!

Better Roads

Once cars became popular, bad roads were a problem. The old wagon routes were not built for cars. They were too rough and could get muddy if it rained.

Towns began to make better roads. Maricopa County set a good example. More than 300 miles of *concrete* roads were built. Builders used a mix of cement, sand, and water to make good roads. The roads ran from the farms to markets. They made it easier for people to sell crops and get supplies.

The first horseless carriage in Arizona was a steam locomobile. Dr. Hiram Fenner had it shipped by rail to Tucson. On his first ride, he ran into a saguaro cactus.

Driving was not easy in the early days.

Charles Hamilton made the first flight in Arizona.

Katherine Stinson was the fourth woman in the United States to get a pilot's license. She delivered Tucson's first air mail.

AIRPLANES TAKE FLIGHT

Arizona's first airplane flight took place in Phoenix. Charles Hamilton was the pilot. People called him the "man-bird pilot." He flew a bamboo and silk flying machine at the state fair. He beat a car in a five-mile race, but he lost a race with the car the next day.

Hamilton was a ***barnstormer.*** He went from town to town doing daring tricks for crowds. He shipped his plane by train from Phoenix to Tucson. In Phoenix, he flew at a speed of 40 miles an hour.

Katherine Stinson was nineteen years old when she did a loop-the-loop and a steep dive in her plane toward the crowd at the Tucson fair. She also took a sack of mail from the fairgrounds. She dropped it at a downtown post office. This was the first "official" air mail flight in Arizona.

First Airports and Airlines

Tucson built the nation's first city airport. Eight years later, a new airport was opened. It was *dedicated* by Charles Lindbergh. Charles Lindbergh was the first person to fly alone nonstop from New York to Paris. He was an American hero. At the Tucson airport, 12,000 people greeted him.

Soon, commercial air service began in Arizona. The Aero Corporation sold tickets for flights between Los Angeles and Tucson. The flight took seven hours and ten minutes. How long would it take in today's jet planes?

There were other new airlines in Arizona. Scenic Airways carried more than 5,000 people to view the Grand Canyon. Scenic Airways also built an airport in Phoenix. Today this airport is called Sky Harbor.

Later, other airlines served Arizona cities. One brought air mail from across the continent. In Phoenix, the postmaster took 15,000 letters to a plane at Sky Harbor. He rode in an old horse-drawn stagecoach to deliver the mail to the plane.

Charles Lindbergh became a national hero when he flew by himself from New York to Paris. Later, he dedicated the Tucson airport.

Scenic Airways flew people to the Grand Canyon. The airline also built Sky Harbor Airport in Phoenix.

Memory Master

Lesson 3

1. How did the railroads help Arizona grow?
2. Why did Arizona towns need better roads?
3. How did airplanes speed up mail delivery?

Communication

PEOPLE TO KNOW
Alexander Graham Bell
Samuel Morse
Alfred Vail

PLACES TO LOCATE
California
Pennsylvania
Fort Yuma
Maricopa Wells
Pipe Spring

WORDS TO KNOW
invent
switchboard
telegraph

EARLY COMMUNICATION

Native Americans in Arizona had several ways to communicate with each other. If they did not share the same language, they used sign language. They used their hands, face, arms, or legs to express thoughts.

Native Americans also had ways to communicate over long distances. They sent smoke signals into the air. These signals could be seen for miles. Runners also carried messages from place to place.

Newspapers

Soon after miners and pioneers arrived, they started newspapers. Tombstone had three daily papers. The *Epitaph* was the most famous. One of its editors sided with the Earp brothers in their feuds. The *Epitaph* had a big story about the shooting at the OK Corral.

Most of the early newspapers had strong ideas about politics. The editors

This was the office for the Tombstone Epitaph. *Look up the word "epitaph" in the dictionary. Why do you think the newspaper had that name?*
Photo by Tom Till

did a lot of name calling. They often called each other liars.

Officers of the first territorial government brought a printing press with them from the East. Later, the printing press was used to publish a Tucson paper called the *Arizona Citizen*. Today the *Citizen* is Tucson's evening newspaper.

Tucson also had a Spanish newspaper. It was called *El Fronterizo*. In Phoenix, Mexicans read the *La Guardia*.

Phoenix's first newspaper was the *Salt River Herald*. It became part of the newspaper that is now named the *Arizona Republic*.

The Arizona Republic *reported Charles Lindbergh's visit in Tucson.*

178

Telegraphs

A company from Utah built the first *telegraph* line into Arizona. It ran to a station in Pipe Spring. The telegraph let people in Pipe Spring communicate with towns in Utah.

The U.S. Army built a longer telegraph line. The wire was strung on poles from San Diego, California. It ran to Fort Yuma and then to Maricopa Wells. Smaller lines were built to connect army posts.

This telegraph line helped the army in Arizona. The scattered forts could get quick messages. Other people could use the telegraph, too.

One Arizona soldier was married over the telegraph line. He could not leave to marry his sweetheart in California. Instead, the bride came by stagecoach to meet him. Her preacher in California read the wedding vows to a telegrapher. He sent the words over the wire to the couple. Each "I do" came back to the preacher.

The telegraph is a machine that sends messages, called telegrams, over wires.

These men are building telegraph lines. Wires would later be strung from pole to pole.

An Important Machine

Samuel Morse and Alfred Vail *invented* the electric telegraph. They were the first people to make this machine. It could send messages made up of electric pulses over a single wire. The messages were made up of dots and dashes. This is now known as the Morse code.

Samuel Morse

Figure out this famous Morse code signal:
●●● – – – ●●●

A ● —		S ●●●	
B — ●●●		T —	
C — ● — ●		U ●● —	
D — ●●		V ●●● —	
E ●		W ● — —	
F ●● — ●		X — ●● —	
G — — ●		Y — ● — —	
H ●●●●		Z — — ●●	
I ●●		1 ● — — — —	
J ● — — —		2 ●● — — —	
K — ● —		3 ●●● — —	
L ● — ●●		4 ●●●● —	
M — —		5 ●●●●●	
N — ●		6 — ●●●●	
O — — —		7 — — ●●●	
P ● — — ●		8 — — — ●●	
Q — — ● —		9 — — — — ●	
R ● — ●		0 — — — — —	

TELEPHONES

Arizona was not far behind the nation in getting telephones. The telephone was invented by Alexander Graham Bell in the East. Five years later the first telephone *switchboard* in Arizona was used in Tucson. The switchboard connected many phone lines so people could talk to each other.

This switchboard helped people make telephone calls to many different places.

Discovering Arizona

Phones in Phoenix

The first two phones in Phoenix were connected when a man strung a wire between his home and his ice factory. Later, a switchboard there allowed for more calls to more places.

In the early days, Phoenix always had more than one telephone company. The people of Phoenix had to buy a phone from each company so they could talk to all the phone owners in town.

The Mountain States Company gave Arizona one telephone system. People could now call anyone in the country or overseas.

Linking the Past to the Present

In 1912, Arizonans had 6,000 telephones. By 1976, Arizonans had over a million phones. Can you find out how many telephones are used in Arizona today?

RADIO

The nation's first radio station was in Pennsylvania. Soon the airwaves were filled with big and little stations.

By 1930, nearly one in five families in Arizona had a radio. That was progress. Young people had fun getting together and listening to music on the radio.

At first, Arizona radios could pick up only local broadcasts. Then KTAR joined the National Broadcasting Corporation (NBC) network. For the first time, people could hear national broadcasts live on a local station.

People gathered around the large radios to listen to radio programs together.

Memory Master

Lesson 4

1. How did Native Americans communicate if they did not speak the same language?

2. List some of the inventions you learned about and tell how they helped the people in Arizona.

What's the Point?

The Arizona Territory grew with the help of better transportation and communication. Stagecoaches carried mail and brought people to Arizona. Mule wagons carried freight to Arizona towns. Newspapers wrote about daily events in Arizona and the United States. People got messages from telegraphs. Finally, Arizona became the 48th state.

More people came to Arizona because of the railroads. Then automobiles became popular, and better roads were built. Airplanes took people to see the Grand Canyon. They delivered mail fast. Telephones also helped people communicate. Soon, radio programs became popular.

Arizona's transportation and communication—from stagecoach and telegraph to airplane and telephone—had come a long way!

Activity

Getting Around

Transportation was important to Arizona's growth. On your own paper, draw a chart like the one below. Gather information from this chapter, the library, or the Internet about these types of transportation. Fill in the chart with the information you find.

	Stagecoach	Steamboat	Train	Automobile	Airplane
Comfort					
Speed					
Sights along the way					
How it helped Arizona					

A Classroom Newspaper

You have read about Arizona's first newspapers. They helped people know what was going on in and around the world. Sometimes they had pictures to show what was happening. Newspapers were also a place for people to write what they thought about many events. Businesses could advertise their products. Farmers and other people would also advertise things for sale, like crops, livestock, land, and equipment.

Create a classroom newspaper that tells what happens in your class or your community. Write articles, draw pictures, take photographs, and make advertisements. You can interview special people and write about their lives. You can write about what you are learning and give your opinion about what is going on in your class, school, and town. Give your paper a name, and share your class newspaper with your school.

Geography Tie-In

Find your town or city on a map of Arizona. Then look at the major roads that lead in and out of your town. Can you tell if railroad lines pass through your town? Is there an airport in your town? With your class, talk about how roads, railroads, and air travel affect your town.

Arizona Reaches Out

Chapter 9

> "I like the dreams of the future better than the history of the past."
>
> —Thomas Jefferson

Timeline of Events

1914-1918
World War I

1929
Westward Ho
Hotel gets air
conditioning.

1939-1945
World War II

1910   1920   1930   1940

1917
United States enters
World War I.

December 7, 1941
Japan bombs Pearl Harbor. The
United States enters World War II.

1929-1941
Great Depression

1942
Japanese Americans are
moved to relocation camps.

Chapter 9

Arizona in Modern Times

Tucson, like other cities in Arizona, is growing fast. Our growing population brings many opportunities like more jobs and more schools. But it also brings challenges like traffic, air pollution, and a strain on our natural resources. What will the future be like? You will have a say in what happens. You are an important part of Arizona's future.

Photo by Richard Cummins

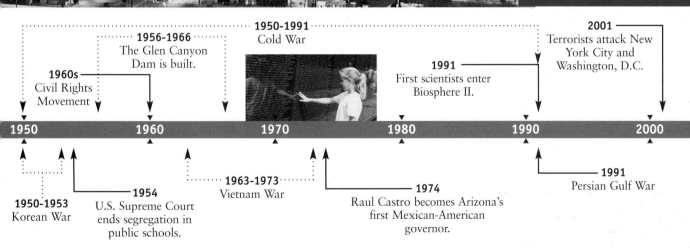

1960s
Civil Rights Movement

1956-1966
The Glen Canyon Dam is built.

1950-1991
Cold War

1991
First scientists enter Biosphere II.

2001
Terrorists attack New York City and Washington, D.C.

1950 **1960** **1970** **1980** **1990** **2000**

1950-1953
Korean War

1954
U.S. Supreme Court ends segregation in public schools.

1963-1973
Vietnam War

1974
Raul Castro becomes Arizona's first Mexican-American governor.

1991
Persian Gulf War

War and Peace

PEOPLE TO KNOW
Frank Luke Jr.
Franklin Roosevelt

PLACES TO LOCATE
Austria
England
France
Germany
Russia
Turkey

WORDS TO KNOW
bond
stock market

WORLD WAR I

Soon after the new century began, a war started. Because the fighting involved so many countries, it became known as World War I. Germany, Austria, and Turkey fought England, France, Russia, and the United States.

President Woodrow Wilson wanted to keep the United States out of the war. But after German boats started sinking American ships, the United States joined the war. Many people from Arizona went to fight.

The Home Front

People who stayed home also helped win the war. Arizonans bought U.S. Liberty **bonds**. They were papers that were worth money after the war ended. The money from bond sales went to the government to help buy things needed for the war. School children in Chandler saved $1,155 to buy bonds. Arizona families also had "wheatless" and "meatless" days to save food for the soldiers. Even children, when eating an apple, were told to be "patriotic to the core."

An Arizona Hero

Frank Luke Jr. was one of America's greatest heroes. He grew up in Phoenix. He fought in Germany during World War I. During the war, the Germans used hot-air balloons to spy on the land below. Luke shot down fourteen German balloons and four airplanes. People called him the "Balloon Buster from Arizona." He became the first American airman to receive the Medal of Honor, an important award from the government.

Frank Luke was a hero. He shot down many German balloons and airplanes.

Peace at Last

When the war finally ended, Arizona celebrated with the nation. In Phoenix, people went downtown. Cars made a parade a mile long. Church bells rang. It was a happy night.

THE ROARING TWENTIES

After the war was over, there were good times across the country. There were plenty of jobs. Americans were making money and buying things. This time was called the Roaring Twenties.

People wanted to forget about the war and just have fun. They went to sporting events and cheered for their heroes. Adults went to contests to see who could dance the longest.

Arizona soldiers were happy to come home after World War I ended.

Cooling Off

Life started to get a lot more comfortable when air conditioners came to Arizona. The Westward Ho Hotel, the Mountain States Telephone Company office, and the Orpheum Theater in Phoenix were some of the first places in Arizona to get air conditioning. Before long, other businesses got air conditioners to attract customers.

Linking the Past to the Present

Air conditioning helped Arizona grow. People could escape the hot, dry desert and keep cool. Working conditions were better, so more jobs came to Arizona. Thousands of homes were built with new air conditioners. Soon, cars had air conditioners, too.

Air conditioners still keep Arizona homes and businesses cool. How would your life be different if you didn't have air conditioning?

The "Frolic" in Phoenix was a popular dance hall during the Roaring Twenties.

HARD TIMES

Many people put their money in the **stock market**. Then, the stock market crashed. Everyone wanted to sell their stocks, but nobody wanted to buy them. Some people lost everything. People didn't have money to buy things, so factories and stores closed. Many people lost their jobs. This time was called the Great Depression.

Hard times fell on Arizona and the rest of the nation. The closing of eastern factories hurt Arizona. Many copper mines had to shut down, and mine workers lost their jobs. Some of them tried to make a living by looking for gold. Farmers suffered when cotton prices fell.

"We ate potatoes three times a day—fried for breakfast, mashed at noon, and in potato salad for dinner. My mother even learned how to make potato fudge."

–A child during the depression

Many families lost their homes during the Great Depression. These children lived in a trailer near Chandler, where their parents picked cotton.

People knew that Roosevelt had overcome polio, a disease that left him unable to walk. They knew that he was a fighter. They believed he could help the nation out of the Great Depression.

The New Deal

The voters elected a new president, Franklin Roosevelt. He had a plan to help end the Great Depression. He called it the *New Deal.*

Part of the plan was to put people back to work. The government hired workers to build parks, buildings, campgrounds, and roads. In Arizona, they planted trees in the mountains. They planted seeds on ranch lands. Some Arizonans worked to build the Hoover Dam.

Lesson 1

Memory Master

1. How did Arizonans help during World War I?
2. What caused the Great Depression?
3. What was the name of President Roosevelt's program to help end the depression?

Lesson

2

World War II

PEOPLE TO KNOW
Ira Hayes
Silvestre Herrera
Adolf Hitler
Benito Mussolini

PLACES TO LOCATE
France
Germany
Great Britain
Italy
Japan
Russia
Iwo Jima
Pearl Harbor, Hawaii
Poston
Colorado River Reservation
Gila Indian Reservation

WORDS TO KNOW
concentration camp
dictator
Holocaust
ration
relocation camp

A SECOND WORLD WAR

The New Deal helped to end the Great Depression. Then something happened that ended the depression for good. A war began. Soon there were many jobs making airplanes, ships, and supplies for the war.

World War II began in Europe. In some places, *dictators* took over the government. A dictator is a ruler who has all the power. Adolf Hitler was the dictator of Germany. Italy also had a dictator named Benito Mussolini. The dictators stopped holding elections. They killed people who were against them. In Japan, an army took over the government.

Attack at Pearl Harbor

The United States did not get involved in the war at first. Then something terrible happened in Hawaii.

The U.S. Navy had a base at Pearl Harbor, Hawaii. One morning in December, Japanese airplanes dropped bombs on the navy base. The bombs blew up ships and killed people. Once again we were at war. We fought against Germany, Italy, and Japan. On our side were Great Britain, France, and Russia.

After the Japanese bombed Pearl Harbor, the United States entered World War II.

Discovering Arizona

The Holocaust

Millions of people from all over the world died in the war. Six million of them were Jews. They did not die in the fighting. The Germans killed Jews just because they were Jewish. Their murder is called the *Holocaust*.

Adolf Hitler believed that Germans were better than other people. He believed the world would be better with only one kind of people.

Hitler's troops took Jews from all over Europe away from their homes. They put them into railroad cars and sent them to *concentration camps*. Many were forced to work until they died. People who were too old, too young, or too weak to work were murdered.

When the war ended, American soldiers went to free the people in the camps. They were horrified at what they saw. The survivors looked like walking skeletons. Entire families had been killed. Some survivors spent a lifetime looking for lost relatives and friends.

In Europe, Hitler made all Jewish people wear a yellow star so that everyone would know they were Jews. Only one of the children from this family—the girl on the bottom right—was alive after the war.

Ira Hayes, a Pima Indian, helped raise a flag during a battle on the Pacific Island of Iwo Jima. A statue was made to honor the bravery of these soldiers.

192

Discovering Arizona

ARIZONA HELPS WIN THE WAR

Arizona changed fast during World War II. New factories were built to make airplane parts. Copper mines and cotton farms did well. Army and Air Force bases and defense factories were built here. Many Arizona women went to work to build airplanes for the war.

Many soldiers from Arizona helped win the war. Ira Hayes, a Pima Indian, was one of six marines to raise the American flag on the Pacific island of Iwo Jima.

Navajo radio men sent and received top secret messages in a code they had made from the Navajo language. They were known as the Navajo code talkers. The Japanese and other enemies could not break the Navajo code. The code talkers saved many American lives.

Mexican Americans served in the war, too. Silvestre Herrera of Phoenix won the Medal of Honor. He fought two German gun crews. Both his feet were blown off when he stepped on a mine. Herrera was in pain, but he kept the Germans pinned down with rifle fire. His fellow soldiers went around the mine field. Then they rushed in to capture the German gun crews.

Navajo code talkers saved many American lives during the war.

People were given ration stamps to buy food.

Ration Stamps in the War

To be sure that the soldiers had everything they needed, the government limited what people at home could buy. They could buy only a small amount of sugar, meat, butter, coffee, and gas. Each family was given *ration* stamps to buy these items every month. The stamps allowed people to get a set amount of food and other items. When the stamps ran out, the family had to wait until the next month to get more stamps.

JAPANESE RELOCATION CAMPS

A young Japanese child wrote this poem about living at the relocation camps.

My Mom, Pop, and me
Us living three
Dreaded the day
When we rode away,
Away to the land
With lots of sand
My Mom, Pop, and me.

The day of evacuation
We left our little station
Leaving our friends
And my tree that bends
Away to the land
With lots of sand
My Mom, Pop, and me
—Itsuko Taniguchi, 1943

During World War II, the United States did not trust its Japanese citizens. They feared they might help Japan. Many of them were put in *relocation camps.* They had to leave their homes and live in the camps until the war was over.

Two of the camps were in Arizona. One was on the Gila Indian Reservation. The other was on the Colorado River Reservation, near Poston.

The camps were set up in blocks. The people lived in small rooms in long wooden buildings. Each block had a dining hall, play area, and a washroom. The Japanese on the Gila Reservation dug canals and grew many vegetables. A school was also started at the Gila camp.

After the war, the camps were closed. Most of the Japanese Americans went home, but many of their farms and homes had been sold. The government paid them only part of the money that they had lost.

People began to realize that taking Japanese American citizens to the camps was a mistake. They realized that loyalty could not be measured by race or skin color. The government apologized.

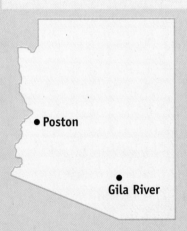

● Poston

● Gila River

Japanese American children enjoy a card game at the Poston camp.

THE END OF WORLD WAR II

World War II changed the lives of many Americans. Millions of people left the towns where they grew up. Black and white soldiers fought side by side for the first time. Women did jobs that women had never done before. American culture was changing.

During World War II, the world discovered Arizona. People who came to the state liked what they found. They liked the climate, the scenic wonders, and the natural resources. After the war, people kept coming. Arizona was the fastest-growing state in the nation.

During World War II, posters urged black and white workers and soldiers to come together.

To end the war with Japan, the United States dropped atomic bombs on two cities in Japan.

Lesson 2

Memory Master

1. What event brought the United States into World War II?

2. What was the Holocaust?

3. Why were Japanese Americans moved to camps on two Arizona Indian reservations?

Civil Rights

PEOPLE TO KNOW
Raul Castro
Cesar Chavez
Martin Luther King Jr.
Wing F. Ong

WORDS TO KNOW
civil rights
discrimination
segregate

THE CIVIL RIGHTS MOVEMENT

Civil rights are the basic rights of every citizen of our country. After World War II, many African American soldiers came home and were denied their civil rights. They had just fought for freedom in a war, and they felt they should have freedom at home, too. They wanted equal rights.

Across the country, and in Arizona, many African Americans were not allowed to go to the same schools as whites. The schools were *segregated*. The black schools did not have many things that the white schools had. Black students at Carver High School in Phoenix had no library, no music or art supplies, and no athletic uniforms.

Putting an End to Segregation

In 1953, a court in Maricopa County passed a law to end segregation in Arizona schools. A year later, the United States Supreme Court ended segregation in all American schools.

Segregation continued outside school, though. Most hotels, restaurants, theaters, swimming pools, and hospitals were closed to African Americans. Signs saying "Negroes not welcome" or "whites only" were a common sight in store windows.

Many people wanted this to end. Martin Luther King Jr., an important civil rights leader, came to Arizona. He spoke at Arizona State University. He wanted equal rights for all people. A few weeks after his speech, Phoenix made a law to end segregation in public businesses.

Martin Luther King Jr. led peaceful protests for civil rights.

Many Americans marched in Washington, D.C. They wanted civil rights for everyone.

Discovering Arizona

Civil Rights for Other Arizonans

African Americans were not the only people who faced *discrimination*. Hispanic Americans, Native Americans, Asian Americans, and women were treated unfairly. They were not given the same chances as others.

Hispanic Americans

In the 1960s, many Hispanics fought for fair wages. They made less money than white workers did. They wanted equality under the law. They wanted to be treated with respect. One of the most important leaders of this movement was Cesar Chavez. He was born in Yuma. He held marches and gave speeches and television interviews to help young Hispanics know they were important. He worked to get Hispanics higher wages for their work on farms.

Hispanic Americans became more active in Arizona politics. They elected people to offices. Raul Castro became Arizona's first Mexican American governor.

Today, many Arizonans celebrate Hispanic culture. They celebrate Mexican Independence Day, and towns across the state have festivals with music, fireworks, and dancing.

Cesar Chavez worked to improve the lives of many Hispanic people.

Mariachi bands are part of many celebrations of Hispanic culture.

Asian cultures are an important part of Arizona. These children take part in a festival to celebrate their culture.

Asian Americans

Many Chinese men came to Arizona during pioneer times to build railroads or to work in the mines. Many of them also cooked and did laundry for other workers. Even though the Chinese usually took jobs others would not take, some mines put up signs that read, "No Chinese Need Apply." The government made a law to stop Chinese people from coming to the United States. Later, the government changed the law and let more Chinese people move to the United States.

Chinese Americans had strong family, religious, and business ties. They fought discrimination with more hard work and education. Slowly, Arizona communities accepted the Chinese people. In 1946, a Phoenix man named Wing F. Ong became the first Asian American in the country to win an elected office. He won a seat in the Arizona House of Representatives.

Other Asian Americans have made Arizona their home. Japanese, Vietnamese, Koreans, and Filipinos are an important part of Arizona. Phoenix celebrates Japanese culture by having a festival called Matsuri. People make origami and perform martial arts.

Native Americans

Today, there are more Native Americans and Indian reservations in Arizona than in any other state. At one time, Native Americans did not have much say in the government. Then, Congress passed the Indian Reorganization Act, or IRA. It was called the "Indian New Deal."

The IRA allowed Indian tribes to have their own constitutions. Each Arizona tribe set up its own government. They were given the right to practice their own religions and tribal customs on the reservations. Another law made it possible for Native American children to go to public schools.

Native Americans used to have to go to Indian-only schools. Today they go to public schools. This Hualapai fifth-grader goes to school in Peach Springs.
Photo by Stephen Trimble

Discovering Arizona

Rights for Women

Women in Arizona and the rest of the nation worked for equal rights with men.

Bosses were usually men, and their secretaries were women. Most doctors were men, and nurses were women. Only boys had school sports teams. Even when men and women did the same jobs in factories or schools, men were paid more.

People worked to win equal pay for equal work. They also wanted women to have the same chances in jobs and education that men had. They wanted to elect more women to public offices.

Many people wanted to pass the Equal Rights Amendment (ERA). They said it would give women equal rights under the law. Other men and women did not like the ERA. They worried that women would have to fight in wars with men. They thought it was better for families when women did not work and instead took care of their homes and children. The vote was close, but not enough states voted to add the ERA to the U.S. Constitution.

The Women's Movement worked for equality and better job opportunities. More women were able to have careers in science and technology. This woman was the first female electrical engineer at her company.
Photo by Bettye Lane

Linking the Past to the Present

Because of the hard work of these groups, we have laws to protect our rights. Laws are important, but laws do not always make people think differently. Change is slow. People still work to make sure that all people have equal rights. How can you help?

Lesson 3

Memory Master

1. What are civil rights?
2. Name some ways that Arizona was segregated.
3. List some examples of discrimination in Arizona.

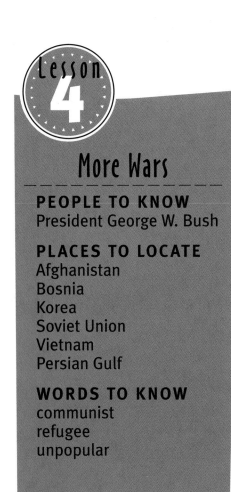

Lesson
4

More Wars

PEOPLE TO KNOW
President George W. Bush

PLACES TO LOCATE
Afghanistan
Bosnia
Korea
Soviet Union
Vietnam
Persian Gulf

WORDS TO KNOW
communist
refugee
unpopular

FIGHTING OVERSEAS

World War II was the biggest war, but it was not the last. Our country was part of the Cold War. We later fought wars in Korea, Vietnam, and the Persian Gulf. Our armed services also fought in other countries such as Bosnia and Afghanistan.

What Was the Cold War?

The United States and the Soviet Union worked together during World War II. They fought together to defeat Germany. But when the war was over, they became enemies.

Each tried to be the strongest country. Each tried to be the first to explore space. Each tried to win the support of countries around the world. This contest was called the Cold War. It was "cold" because the countries never fought each other with guns.

At that time the Soviet Union was a *communist* country. That means the government owned all the land and businesses. It provided the people with jobs, doctors, and schools. The people did not own their own homes. They did not vote for their leaders.

At first, people thought this was a good idea. It seemed like a way to be sure that no one was poor. It turned out to be a failure. In the end, the whole country was poor. The Soviet Union lost the Cold War. The country broke apart.

During the Cold War, this family built a bomb shelter in their basement. They put in beds, blankets, and food in case they had to live in the shelter after an attack. What else do you see in this picture?

200

Discovering Arizona

A War in Vietnam

The war in Vietnam was the longest in our history. Our soldiers fought in the jungles of Vietnam for more than ten years.

It was also the most *unpopular* war. People marched in U.S. streets to protest the war. They believed our country was not fighting for a good reason.

The Vietnam War began as a war between North and South Vietnam. North Vietnam was a communist country. Our country was against communism, so we fought on the side of South Vietnam. The war spread to other Asian countries, such as Cambodia and Thailand.

South Vietnam did not win the war. When it ended, many Asian people no longer felt safe. They left their country. It was a long, hard journey, but many *refugees* finally got to the United States. Refugees are people who seek safety, or refuge, in another country.

Southeast Asia

China

Laos

Thailand

Cambodia

Vietnam

The Vietnam Veteran's Memorial in Washington, D.C. is a large black granite wall. It lists the names of all the men and women who lost their lives in the Vietnam War.

A New Kind of War: September 11, 2001

It was a beautiful morning in Arizona on September 11, 2001. Soon the mood changed. Americans watched in disbelief as they learned that terrorists had taken control of four airplanes and flown them into the World Trade Center Twin Towers in New York City and the Pentagon in Washington, D.C. Americans also learned that another plane had crashed in Pennsylvania.

Thousands of Americans were killed. The first war of the twenty-first century in America began when President George W. Bush and Congress declared war on terrorism. It was a new kind of war.

Far away from New York City, Washington, D.C., and Pennsylvania, the people of Arizona gathered in parks, churches, and homes to express their anger and sorrow. At the Tucson Electric Park, over ten thousand people gathered to show support for the country. They raised red, white, and blue paper to form a huge flag. Arizona people in all towns hung flags to show their support for America.

Americans raised millions of dollars to help families that had lost loved ones in the terrorist attacks. The government increased security all over America. They sent soldiers to Afghanistan and other countries to fight terrorism.

Thousands of people gathered in Tucson to show their support for America. They held up red, white, and blue paper to make a giant American flag.

Lesson 4

Memory Master

1. Why was the Cold War "cold"?

2. About how long did our soldiers fight in Vietnam?

3. Why did President George W. Bush declare war on terrorism?

Discovering Arizona

ARIZONA'S GROWING CITIES

The population of Arizona is booming. People move here to seek a high quality of life. Growth has brought many opportunities. More people bring a wider choice of jobs, schools, recreation, and entertainment.

Growth also brings many problems: traffic congestion, air pollution, and a strain on water and energy sources. These problems threaten the environment and lifestyle that brings people to Arizona in the first place.

The Suburbs

Today, much of Arizona's growth is taking place in *suburbs*. About three-fourths of Arizona's people live in the Phoenix or Tucson areas. Cars and highways let people live farther away from where they work. The areas outside the cities, with rows of houses and yards, are called suburbs.

Suburbs have taken over some of Arizona's best farmlands and open spaces. Many farmers have to sell their land to people who build homes. Building highways has added to this problem.

The suburbs near Phoenix are still growing.

Transportation Problems

People in Arizona depend on cars for transportation. It is the only way that most people can get to where they are going. But some areas in Arizona do not have a system of freeways to move the traffic. During rush hours, the streets are very crowded. All the cars are a major cause of air pollution.

Lesson 5

Modern Arizona

PLACES TO LOCATE
Colorado River
Glen Canyon Dam
Lake Powell

WORDS TO KNOW
suburb

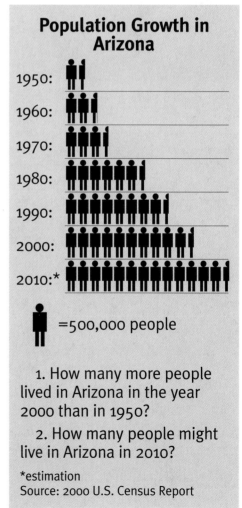

Population Growth in Arizona

1950:
1960:
1970:
1980:
1990:
2000:
2010:*

= 500,000 people

1. How many more people lived in Arizona in the year 2000 than in 1950?

2. How many people might live in Arizona in 2010?

*estimation
Source: 2000 U.S. Census Report

The Colorado River and Glen Canyon Dam

As Arizona's population grew, we needed more water and electricity. Other states needed these things, too. People began building dams on rivers to meet these needs.

In 1956, work began on the Glen Canyon Dam. At first, nearly everyone liked the idea of building Glen Canyon Dam. The water provides electricity for Phoenix and other cities in the West. It also provides recreation. Lake Powell was formed when river water backed up behind the dam.

Other people did not want the dam to be built. They were sad to see Glen Canyon become flooded. The dam has also hurt the animals and plants living in the Grand Canyon. For example, the cold water released from Lake Powell killed many warm-water fish.

Glen Canyon Dam

After Glen Canyon Dam was built, Lake Powell was formed. Many people visit Lake Powell every year.

Modern Pioneers

You have read about pioneers who lived in the past. But there are modern pioneers, too. Right here in Arizona there is a new place made by scientists. It is called *Biosphere II*.

A biosphere is a model of a planet. It has its own air, water, and life forms. Scientists made this little planet using airtight glass and steel. It is like a giant greenhouse. It was built to help find solutions to problems like pollution and the loss of the earth's rain forests.

If you were to walk through the biosphere, it would be like taking a trip around the world. There are thousands of different plants. There are many kinds of insects, and there are fish swimming in fresh water. There is even a miniature ocean. There are deserts, jungles, grassy plains, and marshlands.

The scientists at Biosphere II hope that their experiment will help them learn more about how to take better care of Biosphere I—our earth!

Discovering Arizona

YOU ARE PART OF ARIZONA'S JOURNEY

You have read about Arizona's history. You have learned about Indian leaders, fur trappers, soldiers, merchants, miners, ranchers, farmers, politicians, scientists, teachers, religious leaders, and many others. You have read about choices these people made, and the challenges they faced.

Arizona's history has been shaped by outside influences, too. Wars, the Great Depression, population growth, and modern inventions have changed our lives.

History happens even today. We live in a new century with many challenges. We still need to work hard to:

- protect our environment
- create better transportation systems
- overcome prejudice
- make our schools the best they can be

You are a part of Arizona's history. Your choices will affect how people live in the future. You have a chance to make life better for all Arizonans. Learning about what people have done in the past is a great way to begin!

Modern-day students are a part of Arizona's journey.

Memory Master

Lesson 5

1. How does population growth affect Arizona? Name some good and bad ways.
2. What is Biosphere II?
3. Why was Glen Canyon Dam built?

Arizona in Modern Times

What's the Point?

Arizonans helped our country win World War I. After good times in the 1920s, the country faced some bad times. The Great Depression left many people poor. The government put people back to work with a program called the New Deal.

World War II was a terrible war. Thousands of people died. But the war helped the nation out of the Great Depression. After the war, soldiers came home and started families. Arizona grew. Many people fought for civil rights and equality. After many struggles, the law said all people must be treated equally.

Our country was part of more wars. The Vietnam War was the longest war in our history. Today, Arizona's population is growing fast. We have many challenges to face in the future.

Activity

Heroes in Modern Times

You have read about many important people in this chapter. Many of them were heroes. Some of them did great things to protect our freedom. Some of them fought for equal rights. Some of them saved many lives.

Choose someone you have read about. Research his or her life. Use library books, an encyclopedia, or the Internet. Write a short report. Share what you learn with your class.

Geography Tie-In

Since World War II, Americans have moved around more. Few children live in the same place where their parents and grandparents grew up.

Find out where your family has lived. Get older family members to help you answer these questions:

1. Where were your grandparents born?

2. Where did they live during their lifetime?

3. Where were your parents born?

4. Where have they lived?

Make a list of all the places. Beside each place, list the state, country, or continent where it is located. Find all the places on a map.

Activity

The Census—It Counts!

Every ten years, the government has a census. It is a way of seeing who lives in our state and our country. The adults in each house or apartment must fill out a special form. The form asks questions about how many people live in the house, the ages of the people, and what jobs the adults have.

Census forms also ask people what race they are. Look at the graph to see what the census said about Arizona for the year 2000. Then answer the questions below.

1. How many groups are on the graph?

2. Which group is the second largest?

3. What group makes up 5% of Arizona's population?

4. If you moved here from China, what group would you belong to?

5. If you moved here from Mexico, what group would you belong to?

6. If you moved here from Tahiti, what group would you belong to?

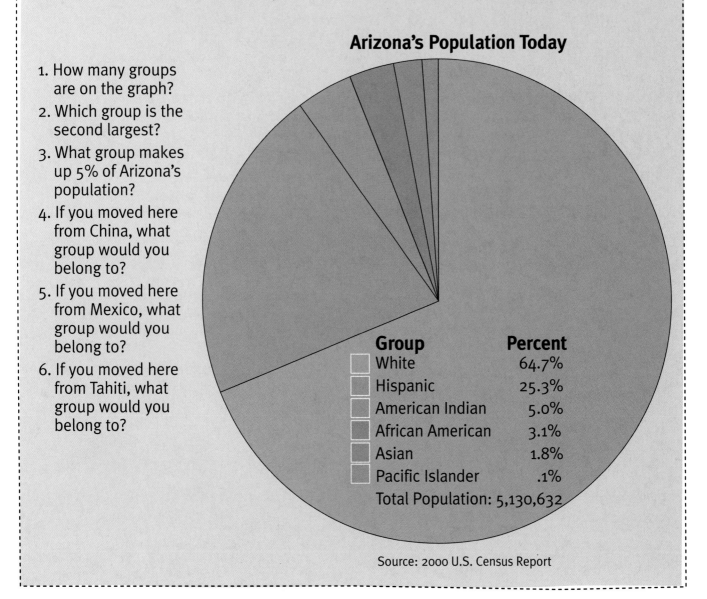

Arizona's Population Today

Group	Percent
White	64.7%
Hispanic	25.3%
American Indian	5.0%
African American	3.1%
Asian	1.8%
Pacific Islander	.1%

Total Population: 5,130,632

Source: 2000 U.S. Census Report

"All labor that uplifts humanity has dignity and importance and should be undertaken with excellence."

—*Martin Luther King Jr.*

Chapter 10

Earning a Living

Visitors from all over the world come to Arizona. They are important to our economy. They spend money at Arizona hotels and shops. Some visitors travel on Route 66 and eat at fun restaurants like this one in Kingman, Arizona.

209

What Do We Need?

WORDS TO KNOW
capital goods
compete
consumer
economics
employee
entrepreneur
expense
free enterprise
goods
labor
minimum wage
profit
salary
services
specialize
supply and demand

What jobs do the adults in your family do? Do they provide goods, services, or both?

GOODS AND SERVICES

People need things such as food, clothing, and shelter. They also want things like cars, books, and bicycles. Things people make for us to use are called *goods*.

People also need health care from doctors and nurses. They need education from teachers. They may need help fixing their car. Things people do for us are called *services*.

The study of how people get the goods and services they need and want is called *economics*.

A waitress provides a service. She also delivers food to customers.

This woman is a nurse. What service does she provide?

This man makes money by helping an archaeologist find fossils. He is providing a service.

The Free Enterprise System

There are many different economic systems in the world. An economic system is a way of making, buying, and selling goods and services. The United States has a *free enterprise* system. Here is how it works:

Most of the factories and companies that produce goods and services are owned by people, not the government. The owners decide what to produce and how much to charge for it. They decide where to do business. They decide who will help them. They are in charge of selling the product, too.

Owners and Employees

Business owners usually hire *employees* to work for them. The owner pays the employees a *salary* or an hourly wage in exchange for work. Most adults in the United States are employees.

What do you think?

Would you rather start your own business or work for someone else? What do you think you would like about each way of earning money?

Government Gets Involved

The government protects workers' rights. For example, some laws help make sure that work places are safe. Other laws set a *minimum wage.* This is the smallest amount that workers can be paid. The minimum wage in 2002 was $6.72 per hour.

Government is involved in our economy in other ways, too. Some laws provide help for farmers. Other laws tell factories they must not put gas, smoke, or waste into the air, land, or water.

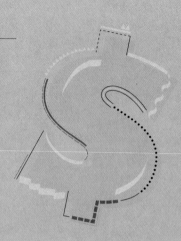

MAKING A PROFIT

Companies must spend money to run their business. A company that makes shoes has to pay for leather, glue, and machines. Workers must be paid to make the shoes. The costs to run a business are called *expenses.*

The company must then sell the shoes for more than it costs to make them. The money earned after expenses are paid is called *profit.* If the business can't sell its products or services for more than the expenses, the owners will have a loss instead of a profit. They may soon be out of business.

If a store has too many basketballs, the balls might go on sale.

SUPPLY AND DEMAND

How do business owners decide how much to charge for their products? The selling price depends on a lot of things. In order to make a profit, the selling price has to be more than the owner's expenses.

The price also depends on how much of the product there is. Sometimes a toy becomes so popular that a company cannot make enough for everyone who wants it. The demand for the toy is higher than the supply. When this happens, the company can sell the toy for a higher price, and people will still buy it. This is called the rule of *supply and demand.*

What happens if the demand goes down, and people don't buy so many toys? The company might sell the toys for a lower price to get people to buy them.

Competition

There are other reasons why a company may lower its prices. Suppose two companies make the same toy. What would happen if one company charged less for its toy? More people would probably buy the toy at the lower price.

Price is one way that companies **compete**. There are many other ways. Companies may make new products or better ones. They may offer better services.

What do you think?

Is competition good for businesses? Why or why not?

BUYING AND SPENDING

People are workers. They are also **consumers**. A consumer is a person who buys things. Anyone who spends money or uses a product or service is a consumer. Are you a consumer? What kinds of things do you buy with your money?

Most consumers want to spend their money wisely. They compare different brands to get the best one for their money. They also compare prices at different stores.

You are a consumer when you buy things. These people are buying ice cream. What are some things you spend money on?

Land

"Land" means anything that is found in nature. This includes things that are grown on the land. If you are making chairs, you might use wood. If you are making bicycles, you need metal and rubber. These things come from the land.

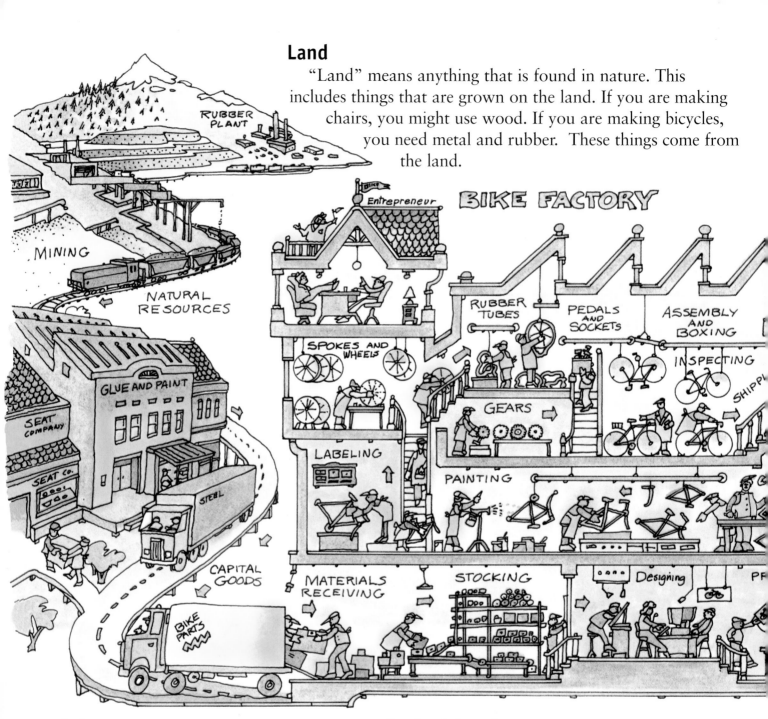

Labor

To provide goods and services, there must be *labor*. Labor is the work that people do. Even if the work is done by a machine, it takes labor to make the machine and to run it. Teachers, ranchers, pilots, dentists, sales people, and farmers all do labor.

Capital Goods

When you use something that is already made to make something else, you are using *capital goods*. The hammer and nails a carpenter uses are capital goods. The tools and paint used to make bicycles are capital goods. The money you need to run a business is also called capital.

Factors of Production

Four things must come together before something is sold as a good or service. These things are called factors of production. They are land, labor, capital goods, and entrepreneurs.

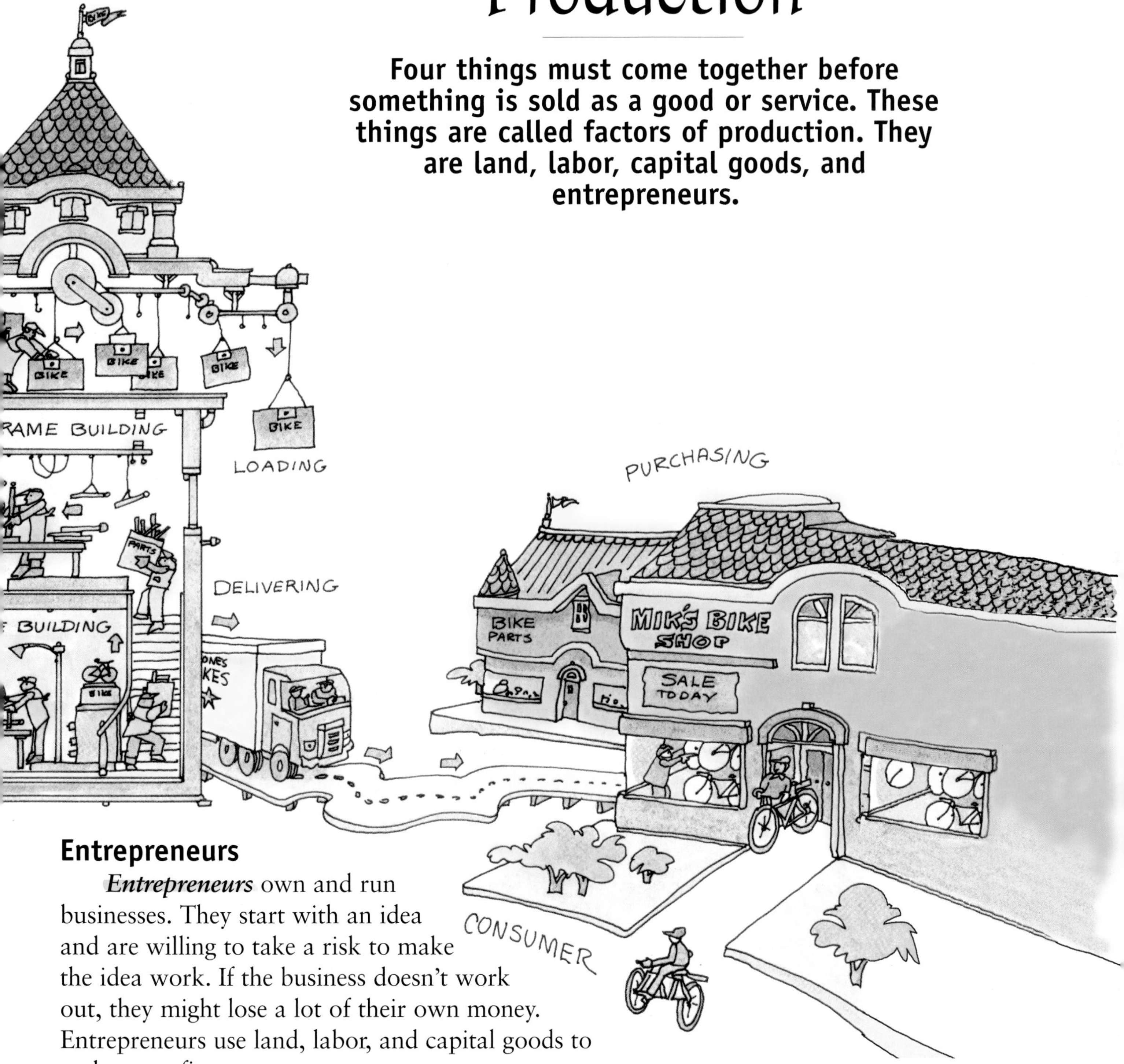

RAME BUILDING

LOADING

PURCHASING

DELIVERING

F BUILDING

BIKE PARTS

MIK'S BIKE SHOP

SALE TODAY

Entrepreneurs

Entrepreneurs own and run businesses. They start with an idea and are willing to take a risk to make the idea work. If the business doesn't work out, they might lose a lot of their own money. Entrepreneurs use land, labor, and capital goods to make a profit.

CONSUMER

Drawing by Jon Burton

Cattle ranches are an example of specialization. They provide one kind of food—beef. Other farmers and ranchers provide other kinds of food.
Photo by Jim Oltersdorf

SPECIALIZATION

One business doesn't try to provide every product and service that consumers want. Businesses *specialize.* For example, Arizona has businesses for mining, electronics, and food. Some manufacturing companies just make TVs or radios. Others make helicopters.

Farmers also specialize. Some grow cotton. Others grow oranges, lemons, or grapefruit. Some doctors just take care of children, while others just perform surgery. Together, all of the businesses provide the goods and services that consumers need and want.

Lesson 1

Memory Master

1. What kind of economic system do we have in the United States?

2. Tell one way that government gets involved in the economy.

3. How do business owners decide what to charge for their products?

MODERN INDUSTRIES

Five major resources help Arizona's economy. They are called the five Cs. Cattle, copper, cotton, and citrus are four of them. The fifth resource is climate. Arizona's mild winters bring millions of tourists to our state. People also move here because they like our climate.

Farming and mining are still important, but many people have moved to big cities and the suburbs around them. There are other kinds of jobs in the cities. Today, a lot of people work in service businesses such as restaurants and hospitals. People also work for the government.

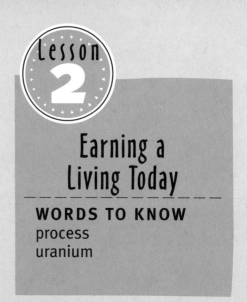

Lesson 2

Earning a Living Today

WORDS TO KNOW
process
uranium

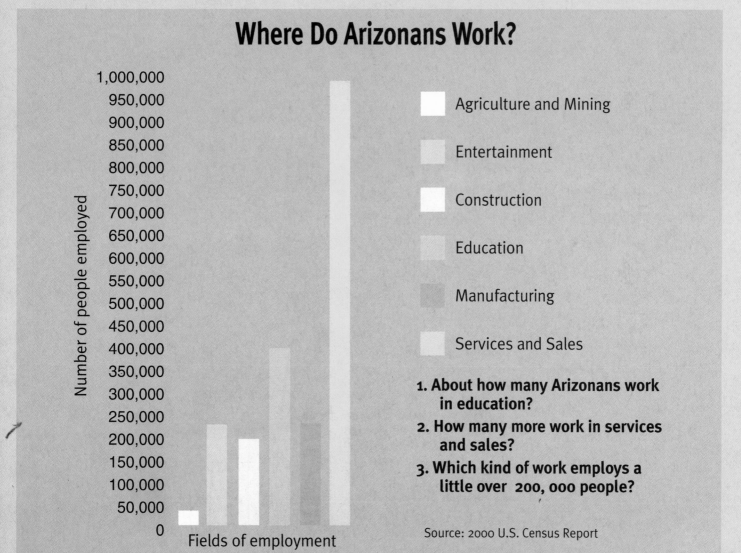

Where Do Arizonans Work?

Number of people employed

Fields of employment

- Agriculture and Mining
- Entertainment
- Construction
- Education
- Manufacturing
- Services and Sales

1. About how many Arizonans work in education?
2. How many more work in services and sales?
3. Which kind of work employs a little over 200,000 people?

Source: 2000 U.S. Census Report

Phelps Dodge has the largest copper mine in North America.

MINING

Mining in Arizona has supplied jobs for over 150 years. Earlier in our history, people came to mine silver and gold. Today, copper and *uranium* mining are important parts of our economy.

Copper Mining

Copper is the most important mineral in Arizona. It is used in goods such as cars, toasters, radios, and washing machines. Electricity travels well across copper wire.

In 1881, the Phelps Dodge company started a copper mine in Arizona. Phelps Dodge has been mining here ever since. Today, the Phelps Dodge Morenci copper mine is the largest in North America. Workers blast apart rocks that contain the copper. Huge machines smash the large rocks. Big trucks can haul 360 tons of copper ore in one load.

Discovering Arizona

Mining for uranium can be dangerous work.

Uranium Mining

Uranium is mined on the Navajo lands. However, the largest uranium mine in the state is inside Grand Canyon National Park.

Uranium mining can be dangerous. Uranium is a mineral that is harmful to people and animals that come near it. Yet uranium has many uses. It is used for nuclear power plants that make electricity.

Some people believe that uranium mining should not be allowed near the Grand Canyon. The Havasupai Indians who live in the canyon worry that uranium could get into their water and make them sick. The mining companies, however, say they can protect the Havasupai and visitors to the national park. They believe they can mine uranium without hurting the Grand Canyon.

What do you think?

Is mining uranium near the Grand Canyon worth the risk?

FARMING

Farming has always been important in Arizona, but it has changed a lot since pioneer days. Farms today are much larger. Fewer people have farm jobs because machines do much of the work. People are still needed to help plant, weed, water, and harvest the crops.

Fruits, Vegetables, and Other Crops

Farmers raise a lot of fruit, vegetables, and grains. They grow hay to feed cows, horses, and other animals.

Farmers grow carrots and onions in the Salt River Valley. They also grow potatoes. Some of the potatoes are used later to make potato chips.

Citrus is the main fruit grown in Arizona. Citrus fruits, like oranges, lemons, and grapefruits, are grown near Yuma and Phoenix. Arizona farmers also grow cantaloupe, grapes, and apples. Most of the cantaloupe is grown near Yuma.

Pecans are another big crop in Arizona. The largest pecan grove in the country stretches through the valley of the Santa Cruz River near Tucson. Pecan growers have to be patient. It takes about twelve years for a crop to grow. When harvest time comes, they shake the nuts off the trees with machines.

Lettuce

Because lettuce makes up half of Arizona's vegetable crop, it is called "green gold." It is grown near Yuma, Willcox, the Salt River Valley, and in other places where there is plenty of irrigation water. Our climate is good for lettuce because we don't have harsh winters or heavy rainfall that will hurt the lettuce.

At harvest time, the lettuce is cut, boxed in cartons, and hauled to cooling plants. Then it is shipped in refrigerated trucks or railroad cars all over the country.

Discovering Arizona

Lettuce is called "green gold" in Arizona.

220

Cotton

Are you wearing clothes made from cotton? Cotton is Arizona's number one crop.

Not too long ago, people used to pick cotton by hand. One person could pick only 200 pounds a day. Now cotton-picking machines can pick 10,000 pounds in one day.

Arizona grows about ten percent of the nation's cotton. A lot of cotton grown in Arizona is shipped to Asia.

Cotton is Arizona's number one crop. These cotton fields are in Coolidge, Arizona.
Photo by Richard Cummins

Ranching

At one time, raising cows on open ranch land was the main part of the cattle industry. Cattle feeding was only a small part of that industry. Now feeding cattle in large pens called feedlots is a big business. Feedlots fatten cattle from Mexico, Arizona, and other states.

Today's ranchers face some problems. To get enough land for their animals, most cattlemen have to pay to use land that belongs to the government. Cattlemen pay higher and higher prices for feed, fence posts, wire, and other supplies. But the price of beef goes up and down. The rancher loses money if he raises too many cattle, and then the price for them goes down.

It takes a lot of hay to feed cattle.
Photo by Stephen Trimble

Earning a Living

This woman is working on a computer part. The electronics industry provides many jobs in Arizona.

MANUFACTURING

Manufacturing means making things by hand or by machine. The pioneers made adobe bricks by mixing dirt and straw with water, putting the mud mixture in a mold, and drying it in the sun. Sawmills and copper smelters are also kinds of manufacturing.

In pioneer times most manufacturing was done in the home. Now most of it is done in factories. Today, manufacturing industries employ many Arizonans.

Electronics

Motorola, a large electronics and communications company, opened a research lab in Phoenix. They make goods such as radios, computers, and phones. Motorola also has offices in Chandler, Mesa, and Tempe. Motorola led the way in making electronics—the first big modern industry in Arizona. Motorola is one of Arizona's largest employers.

Many electronics companies have factories in Arizona today. The Phoenix area is fast becoming a major electronics center. Electronics is a good industry for Arizona. It provides jobs for people at all skill levels. It is also a "clean industry" because it does not pollute the air with smoke.

Food-Processing Plants

Dairy, bakery, and meat-packing plants all *process* food. This means they use milk, grain, or meat to make other foods such as ice cream, cereal, or hamburger.

Spreckels Sugar Company began processing sugar beets to make sugar in Chandler. Arnold's pickle factory in Phoenix makes pickles from cucumbers. Can you name some food-processing companies in your part of Arizona?

Other Factories

Some manufacturing plants in Arizona make products from mine and forest materials. There are lumber mills, paper mills, cement and brick factories, and copper wire mills. Some factories in Arizona make clothes. They make dresses, T-shirts, sleepwear, and shirts.

Discovering Arizona

Aircraft and Missiles

During World War II, several companies built plants in Phoenix to make aircraft parts. Hughes Aircraft came to Tucson. The company made missiles. They also made the Apache helicopter.

Other companies that make aircraft parts include Goodyear Aerospace, AiResearch, Sperry Rand Flight Systems, and Talley Industries. They are all in the Phoenix area.

An Apache helicopter takes a test flight near Mesa. Hughes Helicopters, Inc. made the machine.

Earning a Living

Water sports bring visitors to Arizona.

Snowboarding at winter resorts near Flagstaff is popular.

TOURISTS ENJOY ARIZONA

Each year, millions of people visit Arizona from other states and countries. Some of them are on a short vacation. They come to hike and ski in our mountains, boat on our waters, visit the Grand Canyon, enjoy our cities, and see our deserts. Many visitors have never seen a cactus or palm tree before they come to our state.

Tourists spend their money in Arizona businesses. They stay in hotels, eat at restaurants, and shop at stores. They might go to a local fair, festival, or rodeo.

Some Arizonans work in hotels, gas stations, airports, restaurants, and stores that depend partly on tourists. Many people do not realize how important tourism is to the Arizona economy. Tourism is also good for our state because it helps us to learn about other people.

The London Bridge

London's most famous bridge isn't in London anymore. Visitors come to see the famous bridge in Lake Havasu City. The bridge is hundreds of years old. It was brought here, piece by piece, all the way from London, England. One man paid almost 3 million dollars to buy the London Bridge and 7 million dollars to bring the bridge to Arizona. It took a long time to put the bridge back together.

Every year, thousands of people visit the Grand Canyon.

Earning a Living

Road construction is an important part of our economy. The people who build the roads get paid. The roads help others get to their jobs. Roads also bring visitors to Arizona. What are some other ways roads help Arizona?

CONSTRUCTION

Arizona's population is growing fast. In the past few years, workers have built homes and places to work for over one million people. Carpenters, plumbers, electricians, bricklayers, and others find plenty of work. They build homes outside the big cities. Other crews work on shopping malls, factories, schools, and homes for retired people.

Companies have built their offices in Arizona's cities. Larger cities have banks, government buildings, meeting halls, cultural activities, and places for entertainment.

Lesson 2

Memory Master

1. What are Arizona's five Cs?

2. What is Arizona's number one crop?

3. How does tourism help our economy?

ECONOMICS IN EARLY TIMES

Today, Americans use the free enterprise system. But it was not always like this. People used to trade goods and services. A woman who wove beautiful baskets might trade a basket for food or something else she needed. A hunter might trade animal furs for tools. Settlers also traded among themselves. A family that raised chickens might trade their eggs for shoes. This trading is called *bartering*.

Bartering didn't always work so well. What if a family wanted to trade eggs for shoes, but the shoemaker didn't need eggs? Trading would not help the shoemaker meet his needs.

MONEY

Using money solves this problem. The family can sell their eggs for money and use the money to buy shoes. Today, the government prints our money. Everyone in the United States must use the same money. It's one way that the government is important to our economy.

SAVING AND PLANNING

Money lets us buy different things. It also gives us a way to plan ahead. There are many ways to earn money. Suppose you get an allowance from your family, or you start a business. You might walk dogs or mow lawns.

Suppose you earn $10 each week. You want to buy a bicycle that costs $150. How could you do this? You could save your money until you have enough for the bike. How long would it take if you saved the $10 each week? How long would it take if you saved $5 and spent $5?

Your Money

WORDS TO KNOW
barter
insure
interest

People use money to buy things they need and want. Do you earn money? Do you spend it wisely?

Banks are places to save or borrow money. This bank serves people who live in Scottsdale.

BANKS PROVIDE A SERVICE

Money is important to people. It helps them get the things they need and want. People like to keep their money in a safe place. Most people keep it in a bank. Let's learn how banks offer services to people.

A Dollar Saved

Saving money is as important as earning it. In the early days, there were no banks where people could safely put their money. People saved money in fruit jars, under the mattress, or in a hole in the yard. Today we have banks that are safe places to keep money. A savings account in a bank is safe today because the government *insures* the money. That means if the bank has to close, the government will give you back your savings.

Many children save money to help pay for something they really want. Are you saving money for something special?

Interest

Banks pay you a small amount of money, called *interest,* on the money you put into a savings account. Some banks also pay interest on the money you have in a checking account.

You have learned that a business needs to make a profit in order to survive. How do banks make money? When you put money into a savings or checking account, the money doesn't just stay there with your name on it. The bank uses your money to make loans to other people. Those people pay interest on the money they borrow. They pay a lot more interest than the bank is paying you. That is one way banks make money.

Cash, Checks, and Cards

Today, checks are an easy way for adults to pay for things. They have to put money in the bank before they can write a check to spend the money. Adults can also use debit cards to subtract money from a bank account when they buy things.

Credit cards, on the other hand, are a way to buy now and pay later. Credit card companies add up the charges for the things you buy. You must pay back at least part of the charges each month. Credit card companies charge for the service of lending you money. They add interest to each month's bill. This means you end up paying more for the things you bought with a credit card.

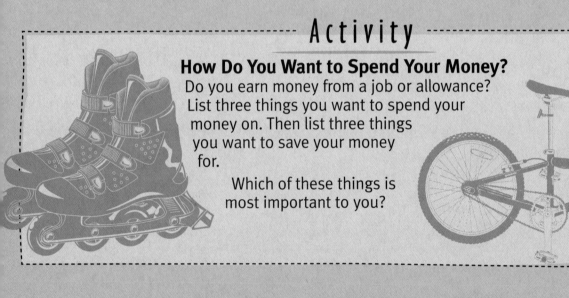

Activity

How Do You Want to Spend Your Money?
Do you earn money from a job or allowance? List three things you want to spend your money on. Then list three things you want to save your money for.

Which of these things is most important to you?

Lesson 3

Memory Master

1. Tell one way that bartering is different from our economic system today.

2. How can banks be helpful to you?

3. Explain how interest works.

Earning a Living

What's the Point?

People have needs and wants. In order to meet their needs and wants, they produce goods and sell services. They participate in an economic system. People work to make a living, so they can pay for goods and services.

Throughout our history, people have found different ways to make a living. They farmed, mined, raised cattle, and opened new businesses. Today, Arizonans still farm and mine. Many work for manufacturing companies and in service jobs. Tourists also help our economy. How do the people in your family earn a living? You and your family are part of Arizona's economy.

Activity

The World in Your Closet
You are an important part of the world economy. Really! Look around your house to see if you can find things that were made in other countries.

1. Search your closet and drawers. Read the labels on your clothes. Where were your clothes made?

2. Look in your kitchen cupboards and refrigerator. Read the labels on cans and packages. Where was the food grown or packaged?

3. Ask adults you know where their cars were made. How do you think the cars got to their houses?

Geography Tie-In

Arizona Industries
For each industry listed below, give at least two examples of a business in that industry. You can use this chapter or the yellow pages of a phone book to help you.

manufacturing   service   electronics
tourism   transportation   government
agriculture (farming and ranching)

Which of these industries depend on Arizona's special geographic features such as location, climate, land, and resources? Which do not?

High-Tech Jobs

In this chapter, you learned a little about jobs working with electronics and communications. These are called high-tech jobs. Do some research. Ask an adult to help you look in library books, an encyclopedia, a dictionary, and on the Internet to learn more about the many kinds of high-tech jobs.

Tell as much as you can about some of the jobs. Would you like to work in a high-tech job when you get older?

When I Have a Job

Someday you will be an adult and work at a job. If you could choose any job in the world, what would it be? Do you know how much money a week you will make at the job? What kind of training will you need?

Make a poster that shows you working at the job. Write about the job and add the writing to the poster.

This woman helps take care of animals. It is one of many jobs you could do when you get older.

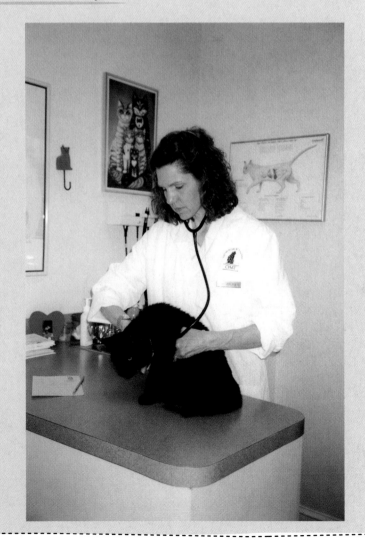

Chapter 11

"The happy union of these states is a wonder. Their constitution is a miracle. Their example is the hope of liberty throughout the world."

—James Madison

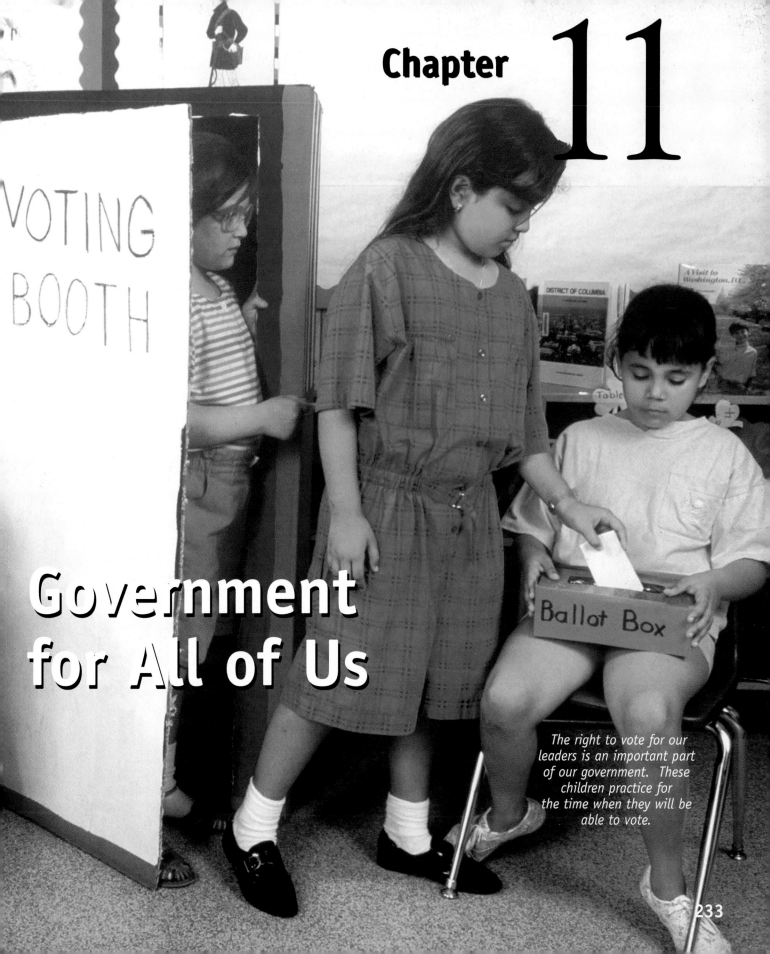

Government for All of Us

The right to vote for our leaders is an important part of our government. These children practice for the time when they will be able to vote.

What Do We Need?

PEOPLE TO KNOW
Alexander Hamilton
James Madison
John McCain
George Washington

WORDS TO KNOW
checks and balances
constitution
jury
legislator
representative

OUR GOVERNMENT

Government is all around us. Government is laws, leaders, and more. Your family is one form of government. At home, there are things you are allowed to do and not allowed to do. The school is another type of government. If you are a Native American, you also have a tribal government.

Why Do We Need Government?

We want roads, parks, schools, libraries, police, firefighters, clean water, and many other services. We want an army to protect us. We want things to be made right if they are wrong. The government provides these things.

The government makes sure we have firefighters. In the summer of 2002, many firefighters helped end a huge fire in Arizona. These firefighters worked to protect a home in the path of the Rodeo-Chediski fire, the largest fire in Arizona's history.

A NEW NATION

When the colonists came to America, they were still ruled by the king of England. The colonies wanted to have their own leaders, but England wanted to have control.

On July 4, 1776, the thirteen colonies declared their independence from England. They set up a new nation called the United States of America. Soon, they were at war with England. They called it the Revolutionary War. After many years of war, America became a free country.

Do you recognize the man standing up? He is George Washington. He was a great leader and America's first president. In this picture, he is helping to write the U.S. Constitution with other men at the Constitutional Convention.

The Constitution

The young nation soon had many problems. The new national government was too weak to solve any of these problems. James Madison, George Washington, Alexander Hamilton, and other men met to write a *constitution*. They hoped to create a stronger country. Their meeting was called the Constitutional Convention.

George Washington led America during the Revolutionary War. He said that the government should be powerful enough to solve the nation's problems, but he also wanted the states to have power. He became the leader of the men writing the U.S. Constitution.

A constitution is a written document that says what a government can and can't do. The U.S. Constitution describes how our government works.

The Constitution is one of the most important documents in the United States. It says that power comes from the people, not from a king or queen. People can vote for their leaders. They choose representatives to make laws for them.

The Bill of Rights

Later, the first leaders of our country wrote another important document. They added a Bill of Rights to the Constitution. It listed rights that the government could not take away from the people.

The Bill of Rights gave people the right to belong to any religion and to speak freely. It also gave people the right to write and print what they thought was important. These were rights that people in other countries did not have.

Branches of Government

The Constitution gives power to three branches of government. Each branch has its own powers. Each branch also limits the power of the other two. That way, no single branch can become too powerful. This balance of power is a system of *checks and balances.*

Look at this giant government tree to see all the important things that go on in each branch.

Judicial Branch

The courts make up the judicial branch. Courts decide what the laws mean. They must make sure laws do not go against the Constitution or the Bill of Rights. The U.S. Supreme Court is the highest court in the nation.

A judge leads a court and listens to cases. A *jury* is a group of people who also listen to cases and decide if a person is innocent or guilty. A judge listens to the person on trial and decides what the punishment should be.

Find the judge, jury, and court reporter. The court reporter writes down everything that is said in court.

Legislative Branch

The men and women who make our laws are our ***representatives***. They are also called ***legislators***. On the legislative branch, find the people who are giving speeches about what laws they want passed.

Executive Branch

The executive branch carries out the laws. The president is the head of the executive branch. Find the reporters asking questions. Find the people trying to come in to talk with the president.

Voting

It is important to remember that the people elect their leaders. Anyone who is a citizen of the United States, is at least eighteen years old, and is registered can vote.

If representatives don't make laws the people want, the people might vote for someone else in the next election. Every vote counts because many elections are close. Find the people voting. Then find those leaders climbing up the tree to serve in one of the branches of government.

Levels of Government

In addition to the branches of government, the authors of the Constitution said that we would have three levels of government. They are: national, state, and local. Sometime the national government is called the federal government. Study this chart to see how this works.

What level of government does the president of the United States work under? What level of government is the mayor of your town or city? What level of the government is our state's governor?

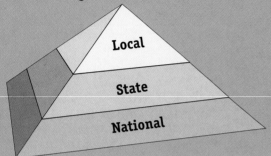

Level	Place	Head of Executive Branch
Local	County, City, Town	Mayor
State	Arizona	Governor
National	United States	President

POLITICAL PARTIES

Adults vote for representatives who come from different political parties. A political party is a group of people who have a lot of the same ideas about how to run the government.

The two main parties in America are the Democrats and the Republicans. There are other parties, too. People who don't belong to any party are called Independents.

A person who runs for office has to raise money, make posters, buy TV and radio advertising, and give speeches. People vote for the person they think will do the best job.

During elections, watch for these two animals on signs. The elephant is the symbol for the Republican party. The donkey is the symbol for the Democrats.

Discovering Arizona

REPRESENTATIVES OF THE PEOPLE

Has your class ever elected someone to be on a student council? Student council members from all of the classes vote for changes in the whole school. They represent your wishes.

When there is a law to be made, each person cannot vote on the law. Instead, we vote for people to make our laws. They are our representatives.

Representatives from Arizona and all of the fifty states go to Washington, D.C., the capital of the United States, to make laws for the whole country. They serve in Congress. Congress has two parts: the U.S. Senate and the U.S. House of Representatives.

The U.S. Senate

Arizona sends two people to serve in the U.S. Senate. Senators serve for six years, unless we elect them more than once.

Every other state also sends two representatives. This means that all states have the same amount of votes. In the Senate, Arizona gets the same amount of votes as more populated states like California, Texas, and New York.

The U.S. House of Representatives

The number of people a state can send to the U.S. House of Representatives is based on its population. That means that more populated states like California, Texas, and New York have many representatives while less populated states only have a few.

Arizona sends six people to the U.S. House of Representatives. They serve for two years, unless we elect them more than once. If our population grows large enough, someday we might be able to send more people to represent us.

Lesson 1

Memory Master

1. Why is the U.S. Constitution important?
2. What are the three branches of government?
3. What are the three levels of government?

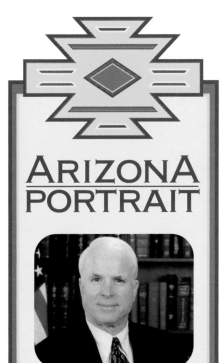

ARIZONA PORTRAIT

John McCain
1936–

John McCain's airplane was shot down over North Vietnam during the Vietnam War. He was ejected from his plane and broke both arms and his right knee. He was held as a prisoner of war for over five years. Much of that time he was kept in a cell by himself.

After the war, McCain moved to Arizona. He wanted to keep serving our country. He served two terms in the U.S. House of Representatives. Then Arizona elected him to the U.S. Senate. He was re-elected in 1998 to serve a third term. He became a respected member of Congress, and he ran for President of the United States. John McCain has fought for many changes and defends the rights of all Arizonans.

Lesson 2

Government in Arizona

PEOPLE TO KNOW
Barry Goldwater
Isabella Greenway
Jane Dee Hull
Lorna Lockwood
Janet Napolitano
Sandra Day O'Connor

WORDS TO KNOW
bill
majority
veto

This is Arizona's State Seal. The governor uses it on all official documents.

STATE GOVERNMENT

The fifty states of our country are all different. Each state has different natural resources, people, and problems. Each state has its own government to solve these problems.

Arizona and Utah, for example, make laws about how water can be used. Water is important in the desert. California's government makes laws to make sure their fruits and vegetables don't have unwanted insects.

Our state government serves people who live in Arizona. Parents have to get a birth certificate from the state when they have a baby. Drivers must get a state driver's license. Doctors, teachers, and business owners must have state licenses. The state government also builds roads and provides free public schools.

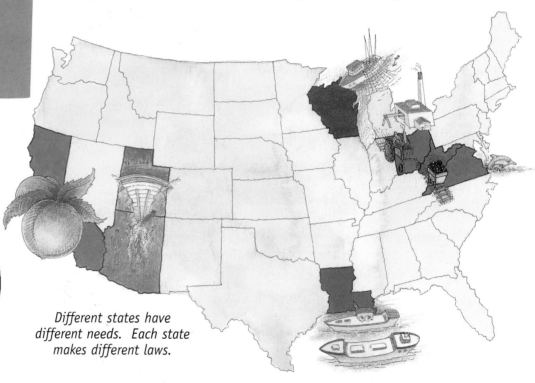

Different states have different needs. Each state makes different laws.

BRANCHES OF STATE GOVERNMENT

Like the national government, our state government has three main branches: legislative, executive, and judicial. The system of checks and balances happens in the state government, too. Each branch does different things.

Arizona's Legislative Branch

The Arizona legislature makes laws. It has two parts: the Senate and the House of Representatives. Arizonans vote for their representatives. Then the people tell their representatives how they feel about problems. They write letters, send e-mails, call on the telephone, or talk to them at their offices. The legislature meets each year at the capitol in Phoenix. They decide which ideas will become new laws.

Arizona's capitol is in Phoenix. Our state legislature meets here.

Arizona's Executive Branch

The governor is the most important person in the executive branch. He or she is in charge of the state government. The people of Arizona elect the governor. The governor has many jobs.

The governor:
- Makes sure that state laws are enforced.
- Chooses many judges and hundreds of other people for state government jobs.
- Tells the legislature what laws he or she would like to see passed.
- Gives the budget—a list of ways state money should be spent—to the legislature.

Janet Napolitano is the governor of Arizona.

The governor can't do all the work of the executive branch alone. Many people help the governor. Some people collect tax money. Some work for our state parks and prisons. Others help with farming, health, safety, or education.

ARIZONA PORTRAIT

Barry Goldwater
1909–1998

Barry Goldwater was one of the most famous Arizonans of all time. He was born in Phoenix on New Year's Day, 1909. His family had lived in Arizona for many years. They were pioneer merchants.

As a young man, he enjoyed sending messages on a radio, spending time with Native Americans, and flying. Later, he was a pilot during World War II.

Goldwater was a Republican. He loved Arizona and worked hard to improve Phoenix and other cities. Arizona elected him to the U.S. Senate. In the Senate, Goldwater became a national leader. He ran for president of the United States. He did not win, but he did serve thirty years in the U.S. Senate. People respected his honesty and courage.

Sandra Day O'Conner
1930–

Sandra Day O'Conner grew up on the Lazy B Ranch in Greenlee County. As a young girl, she was the first female to go on a cattle roundup on her father's ranch. O'Conner later became the first female to do some important things in the government.

She was the first female in the nation to serve as Senate majority leader. Later, President Ronald Reagan made her the first female to serve on the U.S. Supreme Court. She has helped make important decisions for our country.

Today, there is a tall statue of O'Conner standing in a courthouse in Phoenix. Susan Henningsen, an art teacher from Madison Simis Elementary in Phoenix, spent an entire year making the statue. It serves as a symbol of O'Conner's importance to our state and our nation.

The Maricopa County courthouse is in Phoenix.
Photo by Richard Cummins

Arizona's Judicial Branch

In Arizona there are four levels of courts. The state supreme court is the highest. Some courts handle divorces, wills, and cases for young people. Other courts handle things like traffic tickets, theft, or disturbing the peace. A police court, found in many Arizona cities, mainly handles traffic tickets. Court judges can also marry people.

Arizona Women in Government

In 1912, Arizona men voted to give women the right to vote. That was eight years before women could vote in all the other states. Soon after, the first two women were elected to the state legislature. Since then, many women have been elected to serve Arizona.

Many women have been judges in Arizona. The first woman superior court judge was Lorna Lockwood from Tombstone. Lockwood was also the first woman in the United States to be chief justice of a state supreme court.

Isabella Greenway was the first woman to represent Arizona in the U.S. Congress.

Some Arizona women have also served in the national government. Isabella Greenway was Arizona's first woman to serve in the U.S. Congress. Later, Sandra Day O'Conner became the first woman to serve on the U.S. Supreme Court, the highest court in the nation.

Discovering Arizona

How a Bill Becomes a Law

1. A **bill** is a written idea for a new law. Someone writes the bill and takes it to either the Senate or the House of Representatives.

After legislatures debate about the good and bad points of the bill, they take a vote. If a **majority** (more than half) of the legislators vote yes on the bill, it goes to the other group for a vote.

If a majority of that group also votes yes, the bill goes to the governor. If a majority of representatives in either the Senate or the House of Representatives votes no on the bill, it does not become a law.

2. If the governor believes the bill would make a good law, the governor signs the bill. It becomes a new law for Arizona. If the governor does not believe the bill would make a good law, he or she does not sign it. The bill is sent back to where it started. This is called a **veto.**

3. After a veto, the legislators can vote again if they wish. If enough legislators vote for the bill again, it can become a law without going to the governor again. This is one way the power of making laws is shared by both branches of government.

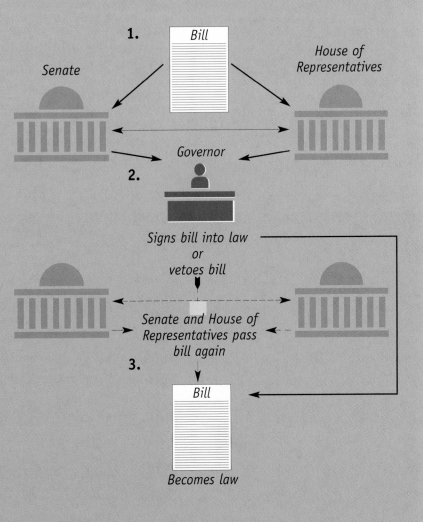

1.
Bill
Senate
House of Representatives
Governor
2.
Signs bill into law
or
vetoes bill
Senate and House of Representatives pass bill again
3.
Bill
Becomes law

Lesson 2

Memory Master

1. What branch of government makes laws?
2. Who is in charge of the state's executive branch?
3. Who has to sign a bill before it becomes law?

Lesson 3

Local Government

WORD TO KNOW
county seat

COUNTY GOVERNMENT

Because people in different places need different things, local governments are important. A local government serves the people in a small part of the state, like a county or city. Everyone in Arizona lives in a county.

Taking Care of Arizona's Counties

The county government builds roads, has a county jail, and may provide parks and libraries. It may provide health care for those who can't pay for it on their own. County officers keep a record of your property and hold elections.

Many Counties

Arizona began with four counties. We now have fifteen counties. Arizona's counties are all different. They vary in size, population, and scenery. Maricopa County has more than half the state's people. Most of them live in big cities such as Mesa, Phoenix, Scottsdale, and Tempe. Greenlee County, on the other hand, has the fewest people.

Each county has a town or city that is the *county seat*. County offices are in a courthouse or other buildings in the county seat.

Most of Arizona's counties are large. Coconino is the second biggest county in the nation. It is bigger than the states of Massachusetts, New Jersey, and Delaware combined. What is our smallest county? What county do you live in? What city is your county seat?

Counties and County Seats

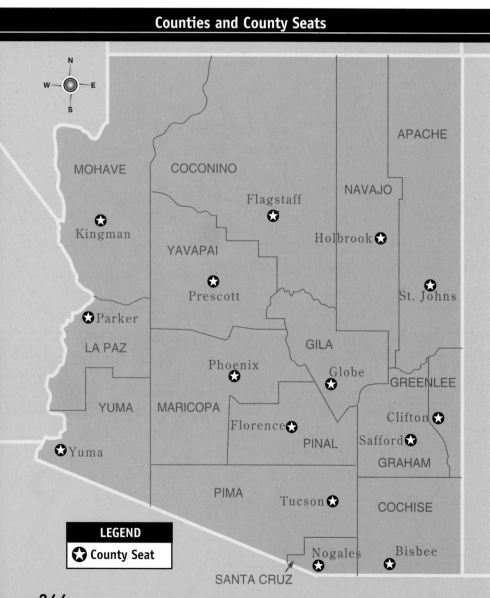

LEGEND
⭐ County Seat

Discovering Arizona

Leaders of the Navajo Nation hold meetings in the Navajo Tribal Council Chamber.
Photo by Stephen Trimble

CITY AND TOWN GOVERNMENT

Most of the people in Arizona also live in a town or city. The town or city government is closest to the people.

The mayor is in charge of the city government. The town or city council and other officers work at the city hall.

Tribal Government

Native Americans on reservations have a tribal government. Most Arizona tribes elect a chairperson and a council. They run the reservation. Nearly every reservation has a police force and a court.

Taxes help pay for the police.

City Services

The services of a town or city government help us every day. The local government provides important services like the following:

- parks
- streets
- street lights
- a water supply
- a sewer system
- fire protection
- police
- garbage removal

In many places, people expect even more from the local government. They want zoos, libraries, airports, sidewalks, swimming pools, and sports programs for children. Many cities provide these things.

Cities, like Scottsdale, provide many services. One service they provide is collecting garbage.

Discovering Arizona

TAXES PAY FOR SERVICES

What is tax money used for? If you go to a public school, local taxes pay for your school building, books, and your teacher's salary. Taxes pay for the roads, clean water, police, and firefighters. They pay for libraries, where you can check out books. They pay for parks, where you can play ball and have picnics.

The government needs money to pay for all these services. It collects tax money to pay for them. People pay taxes on the money they earn. They pay taxes to drive cars and own homes. Did you know that every time you buy something, you are paying tax money to the government? This is called sales tax. You are helping to keep Arizona running!

Your Tax Dollars at Work in Arizona

What do most of our taxes pay for?

Education (K-12)	42%	Corrections (Prisons)	8%
Universities	12%	School Buildings	6%
Health Services	12%	Other	20%

Source: Arizona Joint Legislative Budget Committee

Lesson 3

Memory Master

1. List three things that local governments do.

2. How does the government pay for the services it provides?

What's the Point?

The thirteen colonies won their independence from England. After winning a war for their freedom, they set up a new government. They wrote the Constitution and Bill of Rights. These important papers still guide our government today.

The people vote for representatives who listen to the people's ideas. The representatives make laws for all of us. We have three levels of government: national, state, and local. Each level has three branches: legislative, executive, and judicial. Each branch has a different job.

Governments provide many services. They collect taxes to pay for these services.

Activity

Get Involved!

Arizona's people are important. It is important that everyone—men and women, young and old—be good citizens. We need to understand government issues. We need to help others whenever we can.

Here are some things you can do to be a good citizen:

- Obey all of your family rules.
- Obey all of your school rules.
- Tell the truth.
- Be polite and helpful to everyone.
- Keep your school and neighborhood clean.
- Show respect for other people's things.
- Ask adults in your family to vote.
- Talk with adults about what is going on in government, especially in your town.
- Tell your government representatives what you want them to do (by letter or e-mail).
- Write a letter to the editor of a newspaper to say what you think about the government. Letters from young students often get printed in the paper!

What other things can you do? Make a list with your class.

Discovering Arizona

Activity

Your Representatives

Do some research to find out who Arizona's representatives and senators are in the national government. What have they done for Arizona's citizens?

Discuss with your class what you would like your representatives to do for Arizona's students. Write a letter or send an e-mail to a representative to share your ideas. You can find his or her address on the Internet or in the phone book under "Government."

Geography Tie-In

Arizona's Counties

Study the map pf Arizona's counties and county seats. Then write the answers to these questions on a piece of paper:

1. How many counties are there in Arizona?
2. Which county do you live in?
3. Where is your county seat?
4. Which counties border yours?
5. Which county is the largest?
6. Which one is the smallest?
7. Can you live in a city and a county at the same time?

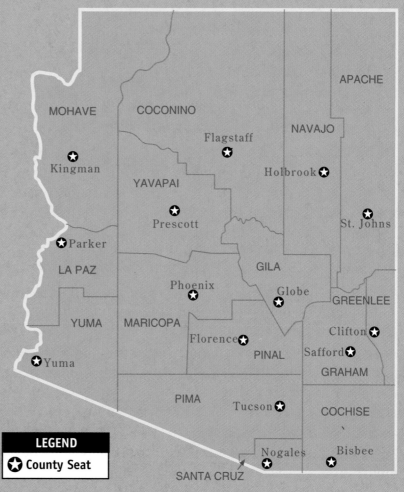

LEGEND
⭐ County Seat

Glossary

The definitions given here are for the **Words to Know** as they are used in this textbook. The words are highlighted in yellow the first time they occur in the book.

adobe: bricks made from mud and straw and baked in the sun

ancestor: a relative who lived before you

apprentice: a person who lives with a master craftsman to learn a trade

archaeologist: a scientist who learns about ancient people by studying the things they left behind

archaic: ancient; very old

artifact: an object made and left behind by people long ago

atlatl: a tool that helped early people throw a spear

awl: a pointed tool used to make small holes in leather or wood

barnstormer: a person who travels around the country doing airplane stunts

barter: to trade one thing for another without using money

battalion: a large body of troops organized to act together; a military unit

bill: a written idea for a law

blizzard: a heavy storm of wind and snow

bond: a certificate sold by the government to raise money for the war effort

bounty: a reward; money paid to a person for killing certain animals

brand: to mark by burning; a label or mark on a product

burlap: a rough fabric used for bags or wrappings

canal: a waterway made by people, not nature

capital goods: things that are already made that are used to make something else

chant: a song or words said by Native Americans in ceremonies

chaparral: a thicket of shrubs, thorny bushes, and other plants

checks and balances: a system that limits the power of any one branch of government

citizen: a member of a city or a country

civil: of or relating to citizens or the state

civil rights: the rights that belong to every citizen

clan: a group of people united in a common interest or relationship

climate: the weather of an area over a long period of time

colony: a settlement or territory under the control of another nation

commercial: having to do with selling and making a profit

communication: the exchange of information between persons

communism: a system in which the government, not the people, owns and runs the businesses and means of production

compromise: an agreement reached when each side gives up part of its demands

concentration camp: a horrible prison camp for Germany's prisoners during World War II

concrete: a hardened mixture of cement, sand, and water used in construction

conquer: to win or overthrow

Glossary

constitution: a set of written laws and rights

consumer: a person who spends money on goods or services

continent: one of the seven large land areas in the world

convert: to change someone's religion or beliefs

country: a land region under the control of one government

county seat: the city where the county government has its offices

crater: a hole in the ground formed by a bomb, mine, or impact of a meteorite

dam: a barrier to hold back rivers or other bodies of water

dedicate: to set apart for a certain purpose

descendant: someone who comes from an ancestor

dictator: a ruler with all the power

discrimination: treating people unfairly because they are different in some way

economics: the study of how people use their resources to make, sell, buy, and use goods and services

elevation: how high a place is above sea level

employee: a person who works for wages at a company or for someone else

entrepreneur: a person who has an idea and the courage to start a business

erupt: to break through a surface; to burst forth

etch: to make a design on a hard surface by wearing away part of the surface, usually with acid

expense: a cost; money spent; in business, the money spent to make a good or provide a service

extinct: no longer existing on earth

flint: a hard stone that produces a spark when hit by metal

fossil: an imprint or actual remains of a plant or animal in rock

free enterprise: a system where the people, not the government, run and own the businesses

freight: a load of goods to be transported; cargo

geography: the study of the earth and the people, animals, and plants living on it; locations of places on the earth

geologist: someone who studies the history of the earth, including its rocks and physical changes over time

geometric: a shape that has straight lines, triangles, or circles

glacier: a large mass of ice built up over a long period of time

goods: products that are made, bought, and sold

habitat: the natural home of an animal

harbor: a sheltered part of a body of water deep enough for anchoring ships

hemisphere: half of the earth, usually divided by the equator or prime meridian

hibernate: to spend the winter resting

hogan: an eight-sided house made by the Navajo

Holocaust: the killing of European Jews and others in Nazi concentration camps during World War II

human feature: changes people make to the land

humid: damp; moist air

hunters and gatherers: people who move around to hunt animals and gather wild food to survive

hydraulic: operated, moved, or brought about by means of water

independence: freedom from another country's control or rule

insure: to make something secure

interest: a charge for a loan

interpreter: a person who explains to people what is being said in another language

invasion: a conquest by an army or group

invent: to create something for the first time

irrigate: to water land by using canals or ditches

isolate: to place or keep apart from others

jury: a group of people who listen to a case to decide if a person is innocent or guilty of breaking the law

kachina: a spirit that has special powers and is sacred to the Hopi; a kachina doll

kiva: a religious structure built by Native Americans, often underground

labor: the work people do

latitude: imaginary lines on a globe or map that measure how far north or south of the equator a place is

legislator: one of a group that makes the laws; a member of the House or the Senate

location: the place where something is

longitude: imaginary lines on a globe or a map that measure how far east or west of the prime meridian a place is

lumber: timber cut into boards

majority: more than half of the people

mesa: a small, high plateau with steep sides

meteorite: a small particle from space that reaches the surface of the earth

minimum wage: the lowest amount of money a business can pay an employee by law

mission: a religious settlement

missionary: a person sent to spread a religion to other people

monsoon: a very rainy season

nation: a people connected by ties of blood or by common language, customs, traditions, or government

native: being naturally from a certain region

natural feature: landforms and other natural parts of the land that are not made by people

nectar: a sweet liquid made by plants and used by bees in making honey

ore: rock that has minerals in it

outlaw: a person who does not live by the law

pelt: the skin of a furry animal

pioneer: one of the first people to do something

pitch: a dark sticky material like tar

plantation: a large farming estate

plateau: a high, flat area of land that can be hundreds of miles wide

poisonous: causing injury or illness to people; containing poison

prairie: a large area of flat or rolling land with few trees

precipitation: the amount of water in the air that falls as rain or snow

prehistoric: before written history

presidio: fort or military post

process: to make something or to get it ready to sell to many people

profit: the money left after expenses are paid

pueblo: a village that has flat-roofed stone or adobe houses built on top of each other

ration: a little bit of something, like food, divided among many people

rebel: to fight against those in power

refugee: a person who flees to another country for safety

region: an area that has things in common, such as landforms or economic activity

relocation camp: places where the U.S. government moved Japanese Americans in World War II

rendezvous: a large gathering of fur traders; where furs and supplies were bought, sold, and traded

representative: someone who acts and speaks for a larger group

reptile: animals like snakes, lizards, and turtles that usually have skin covered with scales

reservation: land set aside by the U.S. government for Native Americans

reservoir: a place where water is stored for future use

retire: to leave one's occupation

revolution: when one government takes over another government; a big change in the way things are done

route: a set course of travel

sacred: something that is holy and treated with reverence

salary: money paid to an employee on a regular basis

scout: a person who searches for information

sediment: small pieces of material such as rocks and sand deposited by water, wind, or a glacier

sedimentary rock: rock that is made of sediment

segregate: to separate by race

services: in economics, work done for another person for money

silversmith: a person who makes jewelry and other items from silver

slave: a person who is owned by another person and is forced to work without pay for life

specialize: in economics, providing a select amount of service or goods

stagecoach: a horse-drawn coach that carries passengers and mail

steamboat: a boat powered by steam

stock market: a system where people buy and sell stocks, or investments in a business

suburb: an area with houses and streets just outside of a city

supply and demand: an economic rule that says that how much there is of something affects how much it will cost

surrender: to give up to the other side

switchboard: a board that has many electric switches to connect telephone lines

telegram: a message sent by telegraph

telegraph: a machine that sends messages by a code over wires

timber: wood that is used in making something such as furniture

toll road: a road that requires paying a fee for use

tourist: people who tour or visit places for pleasure

transportation: moving things from place to place

trough: a long shallow container used to feed livestock

unpopular: not well liked by many people

uranium: a silvery-white metal that is the source for energy at nuclear power plants

veto: to reject or say "no" to a bill or idea

warrior: a person who fights in a war or battle

wickiup: a small shelter made of grass, twigs, and brush used by some Native Americans

Index

Credits

_____

PAINTINGS AND DRAWINGS

Burton, Jon 214-215, 236-237

Dixon, Maynard/Utah State Historical Society 150-151

Hale, Bob 145 (top)

North Wind Picture Archives 108 (bottom left), 235 (top)

O'Kemper, Charles/Salt River Project 62

Ottinger, George M./ Intellectual Reserve, Inc. 127

Peter, Cal/Tumacacori National Historic Park 110-111

Rasmussen, Gary 32-33, 53, 54 (all), 55 (top left), 69, 108 (right), 114, 120, 238, 240

PHOTOGRAPHS

Arizona Daily Star 202

Arizona Historical Society/Tucson 61, 87, 100, 111 (inset) (#59715), 118 (#62230), 124 (#61659), 140 (right) (#18127), 147 (#9176), 148 (top) (#42005), 156 (bottom), 164 (#17714), 165 (#22668), 167 (#48515), 169 (#49716), 171 (bottom) (#62354), 172 (all) (#44318, #15020, #48599), 174, 176 (#455230, #1332991), 178 (bottom), 187 (top), 241 (top)

Arizona Office of Tourism 12, 34 (bottom left), 41, 48, 62 (bottom), 66, 79, 84, 86 (top), 112, 113, 137 (bottom), 152 (top), 160 (bottom), 197 (bottom), 204 (both, right), 208-209, 224, 225

Arizona State Library 89, 98

Arizona State Museum/Helga Teiwes 57 (top left), 60, 64 (all), 80 (left), 85 (bottom), 192 (inset),

Arizona State University 211

Arizona-Sonora Desert Museum 30

Bill Bachmann/RightImage 232-233

California Historical Society 96

Chamberlain, Lynn 42 (top right), 44 (top left), 45

Chapelle, Suzanne Ellery 210 (middle), 213, 231

Clay, Willard 8-9, 18, 36-37, 39, 41 (background), 47 (background), 68

Clineff, Kindra 22, 50-51

Cohen, Eliot 35 (top right)

Cummins, Richard 20, 21, 38, 43 (top right), 92-93, 184-185, 221 (top), 242 (top)

Elton, Richard 13

Frisbie, Charlotte 80 (left)

Gibson, Mark E. 222

Johnson, William H. 23

Kent, Breck P. 29

Kitt Peak National Observatory 86 (bottom, both)

Lane, Bettye 199

LDS Historical Dept, Archives 77 (top), 81 (bottom)

Mark Hughes Postcard Collection 187 (bottom)

McCain, John 239

Morris, LaVelle 40 (bottom right), 78

Mulligan, Steve 34 (top left), 35 (bottom)

Museum of New Mexico 126, 160 (top)

Myers, Susan 201

NASA 2-3, 35 (top right)

National Archives 76 (top left), 77 (bottom and right), 99, 128, 137 (top), 142, 149 (top), 159, 168 (bottom), 171 (top), 186, 188, 189, 190, 193, 194, 195, 196 (right), 197 (right), 203, 204 (left), 210 (bottom), 218, 219, 220, 246 (bottom)

National Geographic Society 65

Navajo Nation Museum 75

Navajo Nation Zoo 76 (bottom, both)

New Jersey Newsphotos 196 (left)

Oltersdorf, Jim 216

Pehrson, Lindsay 42 (top left)

Phoenix Newspapers, Inc. 234

Positive Relations 153 (top)

Rowan, James P. 34 (middle), 40, 153 (bottom), 168 (top)

Seattle Times 200

Sharlot Hall Museum 136 (right), 140 (left), 146, 148 (right), 149 (bottom), 150 (top), 162-163, 169 (right), 172 (bottom), 177 (bottom), 180

Stearns Bank Arizona 228

The Boeing Company 223

The Institute of Texan Cultures 97, 101

Thelin, Al 122

Till, Tom 26-27, 58, 72-73, 132-133

Trimble, Stephen 82, 83, 85 (top), 198 (bottom), 221 (bottom), 245

Union Pacific Railroad Museum 179

United States Holocaust Memorial Museum 191

University of Arizona Library 138, 157

Utah State Historical Society 81 (top), 125

Walter, Sunny 14

Washington Dept. of Tourism 52

All photographs not listed are from the Collection of Gibbs Smith, Publisher.

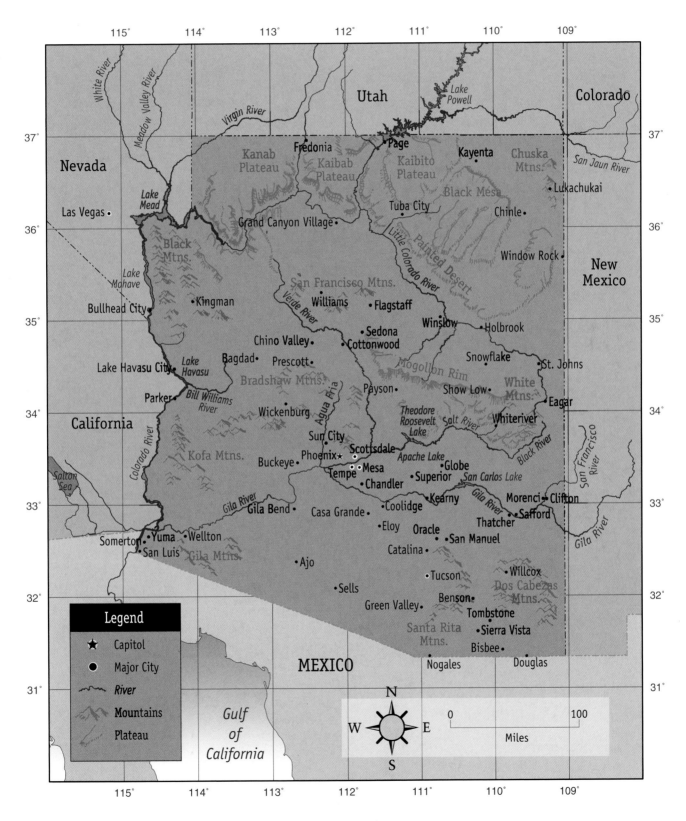

115°   114°   113°   112°   111°   110°   109°

White River

Meadow Valley River

Virgin River

Utah

Lake Powell

Colorado

37°

•Fredonia   •Page

Kanab Plateau   Kaibab Plateau   Kaibito Plateau   •Kayenta   Chuska Mtns.

Nevada

Black Mesa

San Jaun River

•Lukachukai

Tuba City•   *Painted Desert*   •Chinle

•Las Vegas   *Lake Mead*

36°

Grand Canyon Village•   *Little Colorado River*

•Window Rock   **New Mexico**

Black Mtns.

Lake Mohave

San Francisco Mtns.

•Kingman   Williams•   •Flagstaff   Winslow•   •Holbrook

35°

Bullhead City•   *Verde River*   •Sedona   •Snowflake   •St. Johns

Chino Valley•   Cottonwood•

Bagdad•   •Prescott   *Mogollon Rim*   White Mtns.

Lake Havasu City•   *Lake Havasu*   Bradshaw Mtns.   Payson•   Show Low•   •Eagar

34°

•Parker   *Bill Williams River*   •Whiteriver

California   *Colorado River*   Wickenburg•   *Agua Fria*   Theodore Roosevelt Lake   *Salt River*

Sun City•   •Scottsdale   Apache Lake

Kofa Mtns.   Buckeye•   Phoenix★   •Mesa   •Globe   San Carlos Lake   Morenci•   •Clifton

Salton Sea   Tempe   •Chandler   •Superior   *Gila River*   •Safford

33°   *Gila River*   Gila Bend•   •Coolidge   •Kearny   •Thatcher

Somerton•   •Yuma   Casa Grande•   •Eloy   Oracle•   *Gila River*

•San Luis   Gila Mtns.   Catalina•   •San Manuel   *San Francisco River*

•Ajo   •Willcox

32°   •Sells   •Tucson   Dos Cabezas Mtns.

Green Valley•   Benson•

Santa Rita Mtns.   •Tombstone

•Sierra Vista

Bisbee•

MEXICO   Nogales•   •Douglas

31°

Legend

★ Capitol
• Major City
⌇ *River*
⛰ Mountains
⛰ Plateau

Gulf of California

N
W ✦ E
S

0 ——— 100
Miles

259

Washington
Olympia

Montana
Helena

North Dakota
Bismarck

Pierre
South Dakota

Salem
Oregon

Idaho
Boise

Wyoming

Cheyenne

Nebraska

Lincoln

Nevada

Carson City

Salt Lake City
Utah

Denver
Colorado

Topeka

Kansas

Sacramento

California

Arizona
Phoenix

Santa Fe

New Mexico

Oklahoma

Oklahoma City

Pacific
Ocean

Texas

Austin

Alaska

Honolulu
Hawaii

MEXICO

Juneau

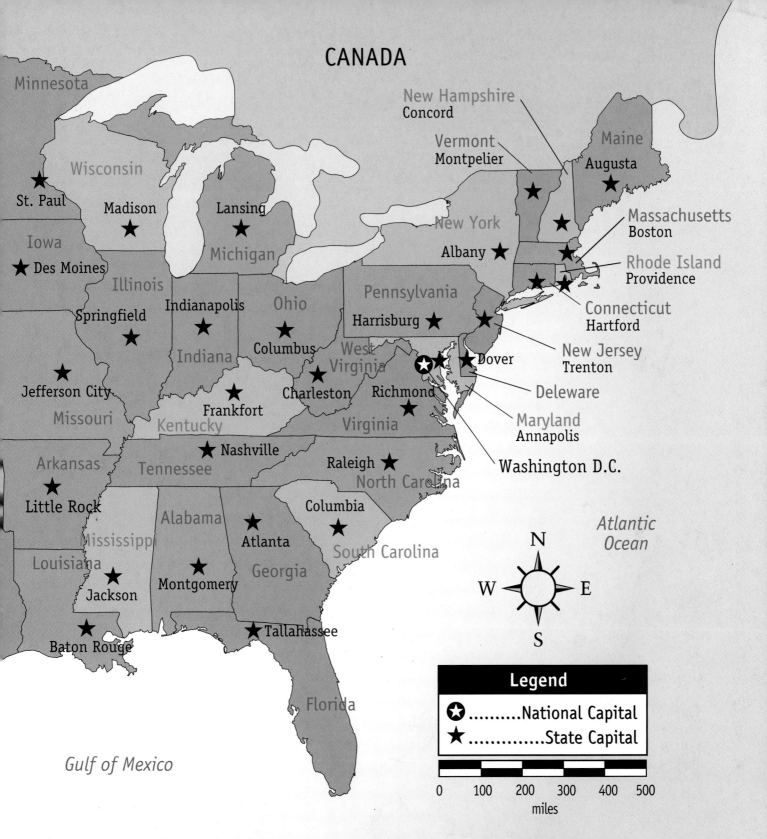

CANADA

Minnesota

Wisconsin

★ St. Paul

★ Madison

★ Lansing

Michigan

New Hampshire
Concord

Vermont
Montpelier

Maine

★ Augusta

New York

★ Albany

Massachusetts
Boston

Rhode Island
Providence

Iowa

★ Des Moines

Illinois

★ Springfield

★ Indianapolis

Ohio

Pennsylvania

★ Harrisburg

Connecticut
Hartford

New Jersey
Trenton

★ Columbus

West
Virginia

★ Dover

Deleware

Indiana

Jefferson City

★ Frankfort

★ Charleston

★ Richmond

Maryland
Annapolis

Missouri

Kentucky

Virginia

Washington D.C.

Arkansas

★ Nashville

Tennessee

★ Raleigh

North Carolina

Atlantic
Ocean

★ Little Rock

Alabama

★ Columbia

South Carolina

Mississippi

Louisiana

★ Atlanta

Georgia

N

★ Jackson

★ Montgomery

W   E

★ Baton Rouge

★ Tallahassee

S

Florida

Gulf of Mexico

The World

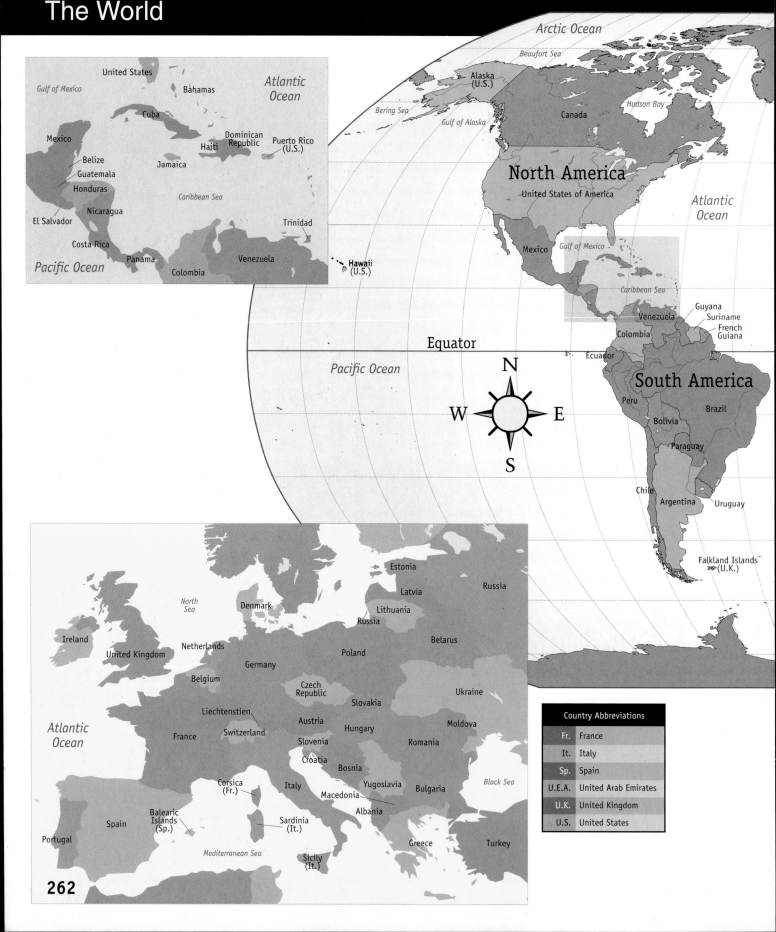

Inset map 1 (Caribbean / Central America):

Gulf of Mexico
United States
Bahamas
Atlantic Ocean
Cuba
Mexico
Dominican Republic
Haiti
Puerto Rico (U.S.)
Belize
Guatemala
Jamaica
Honduras
El Salvador
Nicaragua
Caribbean Sea
Costa Rica
Panama
Colombia
Venezuela
Trinidad
Pacific Ocean

Main map (Americas):

Arctic Ocean
Beaufort Sea
Alaska (U.S.)
Bering Sea
Gulf of Alaska
Canada
Hudson Bay
North America
United States of America
Atlantic Ocean
Mexico
Gulf of Mexico
Caribbean Sea
Venezuela
Guyana
Suriname
French Guiana
Colombia
Ecuador
Equator
Pacific Ocean
Peru
South America
Brazil
Bolivia
Paraguay
Chile
Argentina
Uruguay
Hawaii (U.S.)
N
W   E
S
Falkland Islands (U.K.)

Inset map 2 (Europe):

Estonia
Russia
Latvia
North Sea
Denmark
Lithuania
Russia
Ireland
Belarus
Netherlands
Poland
United Kingdom
Germany
Belgium
Czech Republic
Ukraine
Liechtenstien
Slovakia
Atlantic Ocean
Austria
Moldova
France
Switzerland
Hungary
Slovenia
Romania
Croatia
Bosnia
Corsica (Fr.)
Italy
Yugoslavia
Black Sea
Macedonia
Bulgaria
Balearic Islands (Sp.)
Sardinia (It.)
Albania
Spain
Greece
Turkey
Portugal
Sicily (It.)
Mediterranean Sea

Country Abbreviations

Fr.	France
It.	Italy
Sp.	Spain
U.E.A.	United Arab Emirates
U.K.	United Kingdom
U.S.	United States

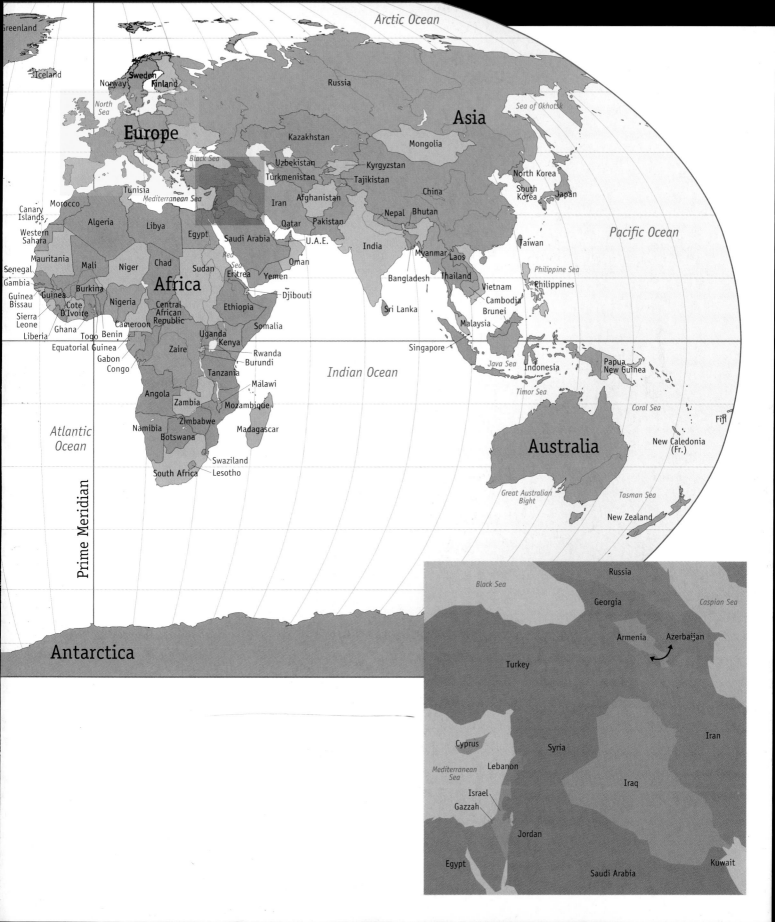